J. ELLSWORTH KALAS

I LOVE
GROWING OLDER
but I'll Never
GROW OLD

Abingdon Press
NASHVILLE

WITHDRAWN

I LOVE GROWING OLDER, BUT I'LL NEVER GROW OLD

Copyright © 2013 by Abingdon Press

Library of Congress Cataloging-in-Publication Data has been requested.

ISBN 978-1-4267-5592-7

13 14 15 16 17 18 19 20 21 22—10 9 8 7 6 5 4 3 2 1

MANUFACTURED IN THE UNITED STATES OF AMERICA

Contents

CONTENTS

CHAPTER 1

I LOVE GROWING OLDER, BUT...

When I was nineteen years old, a small, pastorless congregation in a little town in northwest Iowa asked me to fill their pulpit for five Sundays and also lead them in their midweek Bible studies. When I say that the congregation was small, I mean it was small enough that it didn't expect much, and in hiring me it was expecting very little. I decided to give them more than they expected and offered to hold two weeks of revival services during my time of interim leadership. An elderly widow rented me a room in her home with toilet facilities just a short walk from the house, and I settled in to change the world, one small town at a time.

It's probably significant that I can't remember what I did for my meals. I remember people having me in their homes for freshly baked pie following the evening services, and I think the widow gave me cereal for breakfast. But I can remember only one noon meal, and I remember it because of the conversation. An aged widower had come to several of the preaching services and kindly invited me to join him for lunch some day. I have no idea what he served, though I'm altogether sure it was simple and probably included fresh tomatoes and radishes from his garden. I remember well that he had just two teeth, one upper and one lower, and I watched with fascination to see how he managed with such limited equipment. Very well, thank you. One learns to manage with what one has; and because all of this happened in the years when my part of the world was just emerging from the Great Depression, most people had learned well how to manage with very little.

Back to that conversation with the widower. In one sense it was a complaint. I don't mean it was a tale of woe, because in total my host was a delightful man. This is evident in his readiness to invite a nineteen-year-old visiting preacher to lunch. But the memorable theme from our conversation was on the dark side. He had a word of counsel, by way of affirming a passage of scripture. Shaking his head in emphasis he said, "The book of Psalms [90:10 KJV] says, 'The days of our years are threescore years and ten; and if by reason of strength they be fourscore years, yet is their strength labour and sorrow; for it is soon cut off, and we fly away.' I'm in my eighties," he continued, "and I can tell you that the psalmist was right. These extra years are labor and sorrow."

I am now much farther along in the eighth decade than the Iowa patriarch was when he counseled me, and I want to argue with his conclusion. I will be the first to admit that a very great deal has changed in the intervening years. For one thing, I have most of my teeth, with the help of a bridge or two. Retirement communities are a wonderfully far cry from the county homes in which so many elderly people spent their latter years in previous generations. Social Security has made life much more manageable for a vast number of people, especially those at the marginal level of the economy. Hip and knee replacements have saved tens of thousands from spending their last years in a wheelchair, and a number of medical and surgical discoveries have dispersed many of the demons of aging.

But for me, personally, the old man did a great favor that day. At nineteen, I had not even a vague perception of what it would be like to be eighty; to me, forty seemed like a distant outpost. But I was certain that God didn't mean for a person to look upon any part of life as "labour and sorrow." I didn't know what the psalmist had in mind when he wrote as he did. My faith was sure that whatever he meant was right, but I had the feeling that at the least, the writer meant for us to live in such fashion that we wouldn't allow our later years to be all downhill. I had the sublime confidence that God meant for life to be as good as we possibly could make it with divine cooperation, until at last there was a blessed exit, and that all the intervening years should equip a person for just such an exit.

Which leads me to what I want to say in these several pages: *I love growing **older**. But I don't want to grow **old**.*

Growing older is a process. Growing *old* is a conclusion. Growing older means that you're going somewhere, and that in God's kindness and in your cooperating with God you are taking more of life's conquests every day. Growing old means that you've reached somewhere and that's it. *Older* is a journey. *Old* is a destination. Mind you, I believe in a destination, but my idea of a destination for life is heaven. I want everything prior to heaven to be part of my preparation for that destination. If I settle for *old* as my destination, I will rob myself of some of the best years of preparation for the big exit, the grand eternal journey.

When that exceedingly wise man, Samuel Johnson, heard that Dr. Dodd was headed to execution for forgery, he told his friend Boswell, "Depend on it, Sir, when a man knows he is to be hanged in a fortnight, it concentrates his mind wonderfully." I want to concentrate your mind and mine without the help of gallows. Reaching a certain place in the aging process can serve very well as a mind-concentrator. It's primarily a matter of our deciding that it's time to acknowledge that we're mature enough to evaluate where we are in the journey of life and, therefore, how we ought now to live. This is one of the best gifts in growing older. Unfortunately most of us avoid such concentration earlier in life, and some continue to work desperately to avoid it at any age.

But the chances for such concentration are better every year one lives if one accepts the passage of time as a reminder that there is, indeed, an earthly terminal. This is an iconic advantage in growing older. Not old, but *older*. And here's the point: If we think effectively and productively about growing older, the odds are good that we'll never have to grow old. You see that I'm hedging my bet just a bit because I know full well that we can encounter some diseases that seem almost to change the definitions of life. We'll talk more of that farther along in this book.

If we were very wise, we would begin these studies in commonsense living as early as possible. Of course, something in us simply can't grasp this idea when we're younger. But since life is constantly being extended by the discoveries of medical science and with many people taking better care of their bodies, most of us will still have a good length of time for the so-called later years of life because the period of later years is so much longer than it used to be. And that, of course, means that our preparations should be all the more sophisticated, since our later years probably will extend over a longer period.

Economics is a big factor in preparation for the long stretch, but it isn't my point of emphasis. In truth, most people—even the more casual—hear enough about savings plans, investment programs, the cost of extended medical care, and so forth, that they have some semblance of a financial program in place. It may not be enough, and their financial counselor may shake a head in despair on reviewing it, but in truth the number who are preparing themselves financially for later years is all out of proportion to those who are planning for the larger and more significant facts of growing older. And while it is true that it's hard to enjoy the latter years of life if we're forced to live at a minimal level financially, it's equally sad to see people with money enough to be comfortable who really don't know what to do with themselves to escape boredom, let alone to be happily useful.

If we were all as wise as we ought to be, a book such as this one would have its greatest value for persons in their middle years (whatever that may be in our present culture), but of course the middle-aged aren't likely to get it. They're so preoccupied with getting, spending, hurrying, and achieving that they take little time to contemplate where their lives are going and how they will feel in a few years. That is, if it is important to have enough financial resources to carry one through the later years, it is exceedingly more important to have the emotional, intellectual, and spiritual resources to do so.

I warn you that this book is Adult Reading. I can't define *adult* by specific ages because people mature differently, and of course some never do. Still, this book just might lead an otherwise immature person into adulthood. But it's definitely for adults, for persons who have reached a point in life where they're thinking more deeply about how they are spending life and who now have the good sense to decide to live the rest of it very well. Indeed, triumphantly, as a cap and climax to their pilgrimage.

This book should also be classified as Serious Reading, which means it is for people who are wise enough to laugh at much of what they see, especially themselves. To be serious about life is not to be morbid or pessimistic, but to have a calculating eye as to how best to take captive whatever of life is available to us. To be serious about life is to look at our personal resources in a realistic way ("I don't have as much time left to live as I had ten years ago"), but in an optimistic way ("but I know more than I did ten years ago, therefore I can get more from what's left than I would have at an earlier place in my life"). And at this point where you're serious about life, you stop to chuckle at the wisdom you've just displayed while also admitting that probably you won't put all of this wisdom to work. Indeed, that in some ways you'll be just as unwise as you were ten, twenty, thirty years ago. But remember, you weren't wise enough then to laugh at yourself. You took being serious too seriously.

But you're at the best of all places in your life if you're

growing older while not growing old. To grow old is to grow cynical about life, to give up on people, to decide that life is just one fool thing after another. This is far too gloomy an attitude for someone who is somewhere in the last quarter of life. By this time you've lived too long to subscribe to such nonsense, and you ought not let anyone lead you down that gloomy trail. Human history is a sometimes discouraging study, because we humans seem so slow to learn even the most rudimentary lessons. As a human race we somehow insist on repeating the same mistakes and learning the same lessons from one generation to another. But history is not as gloomy as you think if you read it properly.

Because in spite of all our human frailty and our tendency to keep rediscovering the moral wheel, we do make some progress. In my lifetime we have discovered two fearful new illnesses, AIDS and Alzheimer's disease, and we've read studies in newspapers and assorted periodicals about the dangers they pose for our human race. But with even a little knowledge of history, we remember that these perils do not compare with the fourteenth century when the Black Death wiped out a fourth of the population of Europe, often making ghost towns of complete villages.

Or consider the world of politics. I lived through the days of Hitler and Stalin, and like many I see those names as symbolic of national and international evil. But even the malevolence of such dictators does not compare with the Mongol conquests of the thirteenth century that destroyed an estimated forty million people at a time when the world population was roughly one-seventh of what it is now. I worry just now for the future of democracy as I see the mounting gap between a smaller and smaller economic elite and an increasingly larger group living at the poverty level; the American Dream seems to me to be dying at the hand of greed. But the problem was at least as bad and probably worse in the period of the so-called Robber Barons of the late nineteenth century. If you're growing *older*, you see some hope because you have perspective and you keep learning. If you've grown *old*, you think that times have never been as bad as they are now, and that they can only get worse.

Some of us laugh at ourselves when we get into a conversation where the older contingent tells how deep the snowdrifts were in their youth, when they walked two miles to school, "uphill both going and coming," and how hot it was before air conditioning (believe me, it was!). But these woeful tales are themselves a festival of thanksgiving because in their peculiar way they're declaring that life is better than it used to be! And it is. As I look through the generations of human history, I see times when the pendulum of evil seemed to swing drunkenly toward destruction. But at such times some person or some group of persons pushed that pendulum back the other direction. Sometimes it was a political leader, sometimes a saint, sometimes a poet, and at times a scientist or a philosopher. But always (I dare to give you my theology) it was God at work, using the material at hand, sometimes without the person knowing that he or she was an instrument in God's employ. I believe that God has a stake in our planet and its inhabitants and therefore I need to ally myself with God's purposes. And God isn't on the side of the negative.

Whatever the national or world scene and whatever the economy or the tide of war and peace, each of us has to live out our own lives. This living out of our own lives is the particular business of this book. I say that, not selfishly, but wisely. Because as surely as there is a bad infection that is contagious for destruction, there is also in our world a good infection that passes from person to person and from institution to institution, and sometimes even from nation to nation. Jesus said that the kingdom of God is like leaven: you put a little of it in a lump of dough and its power is all out of proportion to its size, so that it stimulates the whole loaf. I am altogether certain that those persons who live out their own lives with dignity, honor, and laughter hold back the tide of evil and make the world more inhabitable for the rest of our race—including even the villains and grumps and those who choose to stay neutral in the war between good and evil. Those who choose to mind their own business but who mind it well and graciously at least keep the score even, and those who throw their energy into blessing others, even in the smallest ways, are a force for good beyond their reckoning or that of anyone else—except God, who knows all things.

But we have to begin by seeing where we are on life's actuarial table and by falling in love with that location. You can't possibly enjoy growing older unless you make peace with where you are right now. The traveler in *Pilgrim's Progress* discovered that there's a hazardous place in the human journey that he called the Slough of Despond. For many people in their later years this is a Slough of Irremediable Discontent. Such persons spend their time and psychic energy thinking of what might have been: the career choice they should have made, the person they married or should have married, the midlife decision they bungled, the errors they made in raising a child. If apologies will help, make them. If in some measure you can still modify a past error, go for it. Repent before God and if appropriate before a human, but then move on, so that you can fall in love with where you are. And benchmark this hour as the place you will begin, *intentionally*, to grow.

Physical growth comes naturally the first sixteen or eighteen years of life, and mental growth comes naturally and imperceptibly at first. But the most important areas of growth come by discipline, application, and continuing effort. We grow emotionally to the degree that we will humble ourselves to see ourselves as we are. We grow in our human relationships only by constantly evaluating our own behavior and by studying the style of those persons we admire most. We grow spiritually by bringing ourselves under the discipline of prayer, worship, contemplation, stewardship and communion with God.

Now here's the good news. As we grow older we are much better equipped to make the most of such knowledge. We've had enough experience, good and bad, to have learned a great deal. What we know is priceless, because experience is generally a high-tuition tutor. Now we're ready to make our weeks, our days, our hours valuable and fulfilling in ways that would have been impossible a few years ago.

Now and then the phrases of our daily speech are significant. When someone heartily asks a friend, "How are you?" the friend sometimes replies, "Old enough to know better." I'm convinced that you're reading this book because you're old enough to know better. That is, you've lived long enough that you stand on perfect ground for moving into the future. You're ready to love growing older. And because you know this, and intend to live accordingly, you're entering the best years of your life.

Take my word for it, because I'm almost surely older than you are, so I know the territory: enough of it, at least, to have an informed opinion. And here's my opinion. Have nothing to do with growing old—but fall in love with growing older.

CHAPTER 2

THERE'S STILL FRUIT
IN OLD AGE

I'm glad that the cautious word about age in Psalm 90 isn't the last thing that the greatest of hymnbooks said about the subject. I cast a hearty vote for the unnamed poet who gave us Psalm 92. My vote is an expression partly of hope and partly thanksgiving. The psalmist is describing the person who has lived the right way—that is, *righteously*—and he makes his point by using the imagery of trees.

> The righteous flourish like the palm tree,
> and grow like a cedar in Lebanon.
> They are planted in the house of the LORD;
> they flourish in the courts of our God.
> In old age they still produce fruit;
> are always green and full of sap (Psalm 92:12-14 NRSV)

It is the fourteenth verse that delights and inspires me: "In old age they still produce fruit." As we grow older we become more introspective and retrospective. We ask ourselves, as indeed we should, if we've made the best use of our years. If we're reasonable we'll conclude that we've no doubt done some good things, but that we wish we had done more. The next step in our inventory process is crucial. We can conclude that it's too late now to worry about it (and, of course, worry is generally unproductive at any age), or we can resolve that we will do better things (yes, great things!) in the years that remain.

But at this point in our ambitious resolving, we may conclude that we're a bit late. It's too late now to pitch a no-hit game or to win the Miss America title; too late, perhaps, to do much of anything except to keep drawing breath and paying bills. But the psalmist doesn't see it that way. He urges us to remember that one can still bear fruit in old age. There it is, right in the Bible!

We don't know who wrote it or how old the author was when he said it. The author may have been in middle years or even younger; who can say? But at the least this great, unknown soul has done some research. He admires some older people, and in his admiration he looks for a symbol worthy of them—and he finds it, in God's forests of palm trees and cedars. These beautiful trees have a stateliness that makes one think of truly fine and admirable people, persons who have proved as much by the lives they've lived. And best of all, these people are still useful: They are green and full of sap, and still bear fruit in their old age.

I'm not surprised that the psalmist sees the righteous flourishing; one expects as much. But I'm happy that this flourishing continues into old age, and that—especially—it manifests itself in productivity. If there is any common fear-prayer with older people it is this, "I just don't want to become a burden." Sometimes the sentence ends with "to my children," and sometimes it ends without an expressed object, and perhaps it doesn't need one. Most of us simply don't want to outlive our usefulness, or at least, our welcome.

If you pursue such a discussion further, usually two particular subjects appear. We fear that we will be a financial burden to our family or that we will become a physical burden via failing health or disabilities. I ponder the issue in airports, as I see older people brought to the plane in wheelchairs or met by such, or when I see families greeting parents or grandparents who arrive this way. I met the issue often as a pastor, when the younger generation talked with me about the problem of an aging parent, or the aging parent worried to me about how their children were going to deal with the changing circumstances of their ability to care for themselves. As most of us know, this issue is becoming more threatening, because on the one hand our life expectancy is steadily increasing—and thus both physical and financial resources are under greater strain—and the younger generation is currently facing a national economy where one income and sometimes even two is not enough to assist in the support of an additional person or persons.

Those of us who are growing older need to do what we can today—not next week, not tomorrow, but today—to save our families from this problem. Now is the time to change unhealthy habits, lest our children or friends have to pay for our earlier neglect. John Donne preached that no person lives to himself or herself and no one dies simply to himself. Just so, no one should dare to say, "What I do with my diet or my personal habits is no one else's business," because almost surely it will become someone else's business and someone else's time and budget—most likely for some family member, and assuredly for some insurance or government program. It is consummate selfishness to live without thought of what our present conduct may mean to someone else's future. The "righteous" of whom the psalmist writes not only "flourish like the palm tree," they also make it easier on the younger trees around them.

But so far I've spoken negatively, and only of the more measurable elements of money and physical health. The psalmist shows us a more excellent way. We can still produce fruit as we grow older. I have seen those persons who have lived all of their lives with straitened finances because their work was not in the high-pay category, and I have also seen persons who with no apparent fault of their own have become invalid or nearly so in later years—and yet, have been the most cherished person in the family. Their physical and financial measures of life may be narrow, but their spiritual and social resources are such that their value is beyond measure.

This is a goal all of us should seek, and it is a goal within our reach. If we are beginning late in our pursuit, we'll have to speed up our quest, but those who know us best will be grateful for our late compelling urgency. That is, we need to become as good to live with as possible. We need to invest in those virtues and those qualities of person and character that make us nice to be around.

The Bible pays honor to age. There is a mixed picture, it seems to me, in the early chapters of Genesis, when we read of these otherwise unremembered persons who lived hundreds of years and of whom we know only the age at which they had their first male descendant and the age at which they died. The fifth chapter of Genesis gives us an interesting obituary column of such people. The omission of any achievements may suggest that they did nothing particular with their lives; unlike, for instance, an Abraham, a Sarah, or a Moses. But the length of their years seems also to suggest that the Bible sees length of years as a quality that marked humanity when it was closer to Eden. God's will for the human race was length of years, and it has been our misuse of life that has shortened it.

And then there are some great souls. Abraham and Sarah start out on the adventures of a lifetime when Abraham is seventy-five and Sarah just ten years younger. Moses' career seems aborted at forty when in a passion of earnest idealism he kills an Egyptian slave overseer. Again, his life looks at an end at eighty, as a long-term sheep herder. But it is at eighty that his career begins, and all the earlier years are nothing less than prelude for the challenges and victories that follow. The sacred biographer puts an exclamation mark to Moses' story when he writes at the great man's death, "Moses was 120 years old when he died. His eyesight wasn't impaired, and his vigor hadn't diminished a bit" (Deuteronomy 34:7). As for his vigor, I notice especially that Moses objected almost to the end that God should have allowed him the privilege of entering the Promised Land, rather than leaving him stuck on the farther shore.

I'm impressed still more by a lesser known biblical personality who not only was vigorous in his older years but also wanted as demanding a challenge as possible. I'm thinking of the man named Caleb. As a forty-year-old he was one of twelve persons in a special committee that explored the land of promise before the nation of Israel entered. The committee had a unanimous report about the potential of the land. How could they think otherwise when it took two men to carry back a bunch of grapes? But ten of the men saw something else. It seemed to them that everybody in the land was bigger than they were. To their eyes, all of Canaan's inhabitants were Olympic athletes, decathlon people who would be able to outrun, outshoot, and outlast the Israelites. The committee recommended overwhelmingly, by a vote of ten to two, that Israel retreat as quickly as possible to the place they'd come from, in the slavery of Egypt. Even slavery was better than annihilation by the Canaanites.

As I've said, only two men voted to go ahead, Caleb and Joshua, the man who eventually succeeded Moses as the leader of Israel. When you read the committee report, you realize that Caleb was more outspoken on the minority report than was Joshua. A whole generation of doubters died off before Israel entered the Promised Land, and when the time came for the conquest Caleb and Joshua were the only survivors.

For five years Israel made their way into the country that was to be theirs. It was proving a bigger job than anticipated, so Joshua rallied the people to finish the task. Caleb stepped up to remind Joshua of the time, forty-five years earlier, when he had "remained loyal to the Lord my God" after his companions on the study team had "made the people's heart melt," and how in turn Moses had promised, "The land on which you have walked will forever be a legacy for you and your children" (Joshua 14:8-9).

With that background, Caleb made his appeal.

Today I'm 85 years old. I'm just as strong today as I was the day Moses sent me out. My strength then was as my strength is now, whether for war or for everyday activities. So now, give me this highland that the LORD promised me that day. True, the Anakim are there, with large fortified cities, as you yourself heard that day. But if the LORD is with me, I should be able to remove them, exactly as the LORD promised. (Joshua 14:10-12).

I love it! Caleb knows what the calendar says about his age: He is eighty-five years old. But the calendar knows nothing about the state of Caleb's soul and spirit. They are still as young and as ready for conquest as they were on the day a generation earlier when he challenged the ten faint-hearted souls on the committee. And yes, he confesses that part of what the majority said was true: The Anakim, a giant-like people, are at some locations, with their "large fortified cities," and of course the highland is the most difficult land to conquer. All of which, for Caleb, adds up to exactly the kind of challenge his soul desires. I calculate that if the land had been flat and the cities unfortified and the inhabitants fearful, Caleb would have been bored. He might even have recommended that some others take the assignment. But this land, this prize land so challenging of attainment, *this* is just the thing for a leader of eighty-five years whose strength is as it was when he was forty!

In truth, I don't know if Caleb was as physically powerful as he had been a generation before. As optimistic as I am, I nevertheless find it hard to imagine that this man in his mid-eighties is still as quick on foot and can still carry at full speed the weight of ancient armor, but I'm glad that *he* thought so.

And of this I'm certain: Caleb was now a wiser man than he was at forty. I often ponder the wisdom of the sports page. The veteran baseball pitcher comes back for another year. "My fast ball has lost a little of its hop, but I know better how to 'locate' it; I rely more on my head and less on my arm." This kind of reasoning applies to almost every phase of our lives. As we grow older, most of us (unlike Moses) lose some of our naive, youthful skills, but the increase in maturity of outlook, experience, and judgment more than make up for the loss.

But of course the degree to which this is true depends upon how we use the earlier years of our lives—perhaps especially the time beginning in our mid-fifties. We've learned that there is more to life than sheer talent, more than formal education, and more even than experience. There are such issues as judgment, patience, and the ability to listen and to evaluate the data that comes to us. The race is not always to the swift; it is also to those who know the track.

And so with Caleb. Those on his team may have run faster and thrown their spears with greater velocity, but none could surpass him in unbridled courage and optimism. He had reasoned with those who imbibed pessimism and he had known the dull years of wilderness wandering. Life had sketched a background on his canvass that was perfect for a portrait of achieving.

The unknown poet who gave us Psalm 92 was in the Caleb mood. He's not a pioneer marching into new hills and valleys like Caleb, but he intends to take all of life conquest. With a *flourish*. So it is that this edition of the Bible puts it: "flourish like the palm tree . . . flourish in the courts of our God" (Psalm 92:12-13 NRSV). This is no mere survival, no day-to-day grind, but rather a life of sweeping gestures, rolling laughter, and grand accomplishments.

But neither is it a life of happenstance. The psalmist is talking about a particular kind of person, the *righteous*. That is, this is the description of persons who are living the *right* way. We have grown so accustomed to thinking of *righteous* as a religious word that we forget what it means in its root sense, and certainly what the ancient poet had in mind when he spoke of a righteous person. To be righteous is to live rightly, in the way that makes sense out of life. Life certainly makes more sense if one believes that honesty is better than deception, love better than hate, peace to be preferred over war. The inspired psalmist is sure that those who live right flourish; they have the grandeur and beauty of the palm and the cedar.

And best of all, for those of us who believe in aging well, they still bear fruit in old age! This, too, makes simple good sense. If we use our automobile rightly we expect it to be good in old age. Why not also this human life, this life of ours that is made for righteous living?

Mind you, this has nothing particular to do with economic, athletic, political or social success, nor is it an ironclad case for good health—though in all these areas one can expect that the odds are with doing right rather than doing wrong. But it has everything to do with our inner character and our relationship with God. Herein is the essence of right living, a life that is consistent with the character of the Lord God.

I am an exceedingly fortunate human being, in that I have known righteous people for as far back as I can remember. I can see them still, from the days when I was a fidgety eight- or nine-year-old in a little Methodist church in Iowa, through the several churches where I have been the minister and the hundreds where I have been a guest preacher. I have my own company of saints, and if I could name them all they would number in the thousands. The best of the lot are those in old age. They still bear fruit, because they're growing older without growing old.

Of such is the Kingdom of Heaven. And of such is the best of planet earth.

CHAPTER 3

"THERE'S NO FOOL
LIKE AN OLD FOOL"

The title for our previous chapter came from the Bible.
This one comes from secular wisdom, the quite direct,
old-fashioned kind. My mother, like many of her generation,
quoted freely and frequently from a wide collection of
homely proverbs. I thought that "There's no fool like an old

fool" was something she had picked up from her mother or grandmother—which in fact was probably the case. But when I did research in my faithful copy of *Oxford Dictionary of Quotations*, I discovered that the proverb dates from the sixteenth century, so it goes back through a great many grandmothers.

And while the pungent phrase doesn't appear in the Scriptures, the Scriptures provide us with some notable examples. Quite painful ones, in fact.

I assure you that there's no contradiction between chapters two and three. Old age is a perfect time to be fruitful, but it's also a time when we're in danger of playing the fool. These ideas are sides of the same coin. As we grow older we ought, of course, to grow wiser; the breadth and depth of experience almost force us to increased wisdom. One has to be a very dull student to grow older without growing at least a little bit wiser. But wisdom, ironically, can feed on itself, so that we come to feel we're above error, which is a very unwise conclusion. Wisdom ought above all things to teach us humility. Humility is a virtue, however, which involves wisdom of a more-than-worldly kind, a virtue which is hard to gain and even harder to keep. And, of course, sometimes other people help us lose our judgment. If enough people tell us how much they appreciate our wisdom, we will begin to get a sense of infallibility. Most of us don't need many votes to convince us. Two or three will do. This feeling is the burial ground of sound judgment because it prevents us from hearing any voice other than our own, including voices either human or divine. Have no doubt about it: All of us are especially sensitive to foolish decisions as we grow older, and the very qualities that make us wiser also make us more susceptible to such fallibility. That's why older people, in the midst of a discussion, easily interject the phrase, "When you've lived as long as I have, you'll know better." Obviously this statement tends to silence all other statements if we're the oldest person in the room; that is, as long as length of life is the primary measure of wisdom. And with that silence, the older person is ensconced on the throne of infallibility, a place from which disaster is almost inevitable.

The Old Testament not only gives us examples of aged foolishness, it gives royal examples. Take King Uzziah, who became King of Judah when he was only sixteen and reigned for fifty-two years. He enjoyed victory after victory during those years. He received the highest vote from the biblical historian: "He did what was right in the LORD's eyes" (2 Chronicles 26:4). The chronicler proceeds to give us a very impressive summary of Uzziah's achievements, one of the most complete of its kind in the books of the Kings and Chronicles. "And so Uzziah's fame spread far and wide, because he had received wonderful help until he became powerful" (26:15).

Our English translation rightly begins a new paragraph at this point, but the Hebrew moves without a pause to this sad word: "But as soon as he became powerful, he grew so

arrogant that he acted corruptly" (26:16). The king went
into the temple, to perform acts which were restricted only to
the priests. He was smitten with leprosy, and lived the last
years of his life "in a separate house . . . barred from the
LORD's temple" (26:21). His son carried on the administrative responsibilities until Uzziah's death. At the point in
Uzziah's life when he should have been at his best, offering
the most effective leadership and doing the most for his
nation, he was essentially out of office. He had grown older
but certainly not wiser.

And of course there's David. Israel had no greater king
than David. He became the measure for all those who followed him to the throne. He sinned at times, there's no doubt
about that. But he had an admirable capacity for acknowl-
edging when he was wrong, and he desired above all to
please God. Nevertheless, he is among those who played the
fool in his last days; and worse yet, he did so in a reprise of
some of his noblest moments.

Let me tell you the story from the beginning. Well into
David's reign as King of Israel, he suffered a devastating blow
involving his son, Absalom, the son who at one time seemed the
most promising member of the royal family. He was strikingly
handsome, son of a princess, and politically savvy. Thus, when
he felt alienated from his father he used his political instincts to
put together a palace coup. He did it so well that he got some
of his father's key administrative and military personnel on his
side, forcing David and those loyal to him to flee the palace.

When a person of power is on the run, old enemies quickly join the pursuit or the celebration. Among these was Shimei, a distant relative of the late King Saul. As David and his cohorts fled, Shimei stood by the roadside, throwing rocks and dirt at him, calling him a murderer, and "despicable" (2 Samuel 16:7) One of David's guards asked permission to kill Shimei but David forbade him. David said, "Listen! My own son, one of my very own children, wants me dead. This Benjaminite can only feel the same—only more! Leave him alone. And let him curse, because the LORD told him to. Perhaps the LORD will see my distress; perhaps the LORD will repay me with good for this cursing today" (16:11-12).

In the midst of defeat and public shame, David was at his finest.

A few days later, David's character proved its quality even better. His forces had brought the revolt under control (though at a great price), and David was once more secure on his throne. One of the first to offer congratulations was Shimei, the man who had cursed David when he thought the king was going down for the count. Now he fell at David's feet. "May my master not hold me guilty or remember your servant's wrongdoing that day my master the king left Jerusalem. Please forget about it, Your Majesty, because your servant knows that I have sinned. But look, I am the first person from the entire family of Joseph to come down today and meet my master the king" (2 Samuel 19:19-20).

If you've done a quick count you find something like eight

references either to David's position or Shimei's obeisance. It's a bit much, but of course Shimei is appealing for his life; he now realizes that he has played the fool both in judgment and in words and actions.

David's attendant again thinks Shimei is better dead than alive and reminds the king that Shimei should be put to death for cursing the Lord's anointed. David, however, shows his godly character. "Should anyone in Israel be put to death today?" he answered. "Don't I know that today I am again king over Israel" (2 Samuel 19:22). David knew who he was. He didn't have to destroy anyone to prove that he was king.

I wish the story ended there. I'd like for my last picture of one of the Bible's finest characters to be a study in nobility. Unfortunately, David grew old and with his age came a mixture of wisdom and pettiness. It's hard to imagine that such contrary counsel could come from the same lips. David prefaces his farewell counsel to his successor, Solomon, urging him to walk in God's ways and to observes God's laws, commands, and judgments: "In this way you will succeed in whatever you do and wherever you go" (1 Kings 2:3). Then, in a list of details, this:

> Now as for this Shimei, Gera's son—a Benjaminite from Bahurim—who is with you, he cursed me viciously when I went to Mahanaim. When he came down to meet me at the Jordan, I swore to him by the LORD, 'Surely I won't execute you with the sword.' But you don't need to excuse him. You are wise and know what to do to him. Give him a violent death. (1 Kings 2:8-9)

Those are the last recorded words of David, and they aren't the words on which I want him to make his exit.

What has happened? Years before, David knew who he was; he knew he was king and he didn't have to execute anyone to convince himself of his office. Now he has grown old—not *older*, but *old*—and he has given up the throne. He no longer has sufficient body heat to fall asleep in comfort and he has already passed the scepter to Solomon. All that is left now is an urge for revenge, revenge on a poor fool who is hardly worth mentioning. In taking revenge, David reduces himself to Shimei's level. Now David is playing the fool.

And here's the sorriest part of the story. Shimei couldn't make a fool of David years before when he mocked the king along the roadside. Shimei looked ridiculous in his playground showboating while David looked kingly in maintaining his dignity. But at the end, Shimei wins. Solomon will find opportunity in time to order Shimei's execution, but Shimei will have been able to do in his death what he couldn't do with his dirt and stones and curses: He can make David look pathetic and petty.

Here is fair warning for all of us, since all of us have the unfortunate capacity to harbor a grudge. A grudge (and with it, a hunger for revenge) is bad stuff to hide away in some dark corner of the soul during our days of strength. When our bodies are less strong and our self esteem susceptible, we may decide to resurrect the grudge not only to its ugly size but to enlarge it to a place where it can do real harm. And we'll prove the adage my mother loved to quote: "There's no fool like an old fool."

And then there's David's son, the essence of wisdom, the last person we'd expect to play the fool: Solomon, the wisest man that ever lived. (See 1 Kings 3:12.) If ever a young man had everything going for him, it was Solomon. Cherished son of a great king, ordained to the throne by his father and by God, he then received an endowment that every king, president, prime minister, governor, mayor, college president, or corporate executive could long for: God gave him the gift of wisdom, so he could fulfill his assignment with justice and insight. Any person who rises to the executive level can take courses in Administration and in Decision-Making 101. But wisdom? That's something else again, and while one can pick up some of wisdom's salient parts by way of experience, there are instincts for wisdom that seem simply to be a gift. God gave Solomon that gift.

But as Solomon grew older he did not grow wiser. He had an eye for beauty—beauty in gardens and books and horses and the wonders of nature, and in women. Especially, in women. Add to that the quality of the exotic—women of another culture, with a different cast of eye, another texture of hair, an enticing carriage not known to the women of Israel—and he was easily smitten. First Solomon married Pharaoh's daughter, which may have been something of a political act, to guarantee peace with a major military power. But then he "loved many foreign women," women who "came from the nations that the LORD had commanded the Israelites about: 'Don't intermarry with them. They will definitely turn your heart toward their gods'" (1 Kings 11:1-2).

Solomon did intermarry, and the women he married did turn his heart toward their gods. The biblical writer uses the key phrase three times in one paragraph. The king to whom God had spoken with such clarity when Solomon was young and in whom God had invested so much, of him it is said that when he "grew old, his wives turned his heart after other gods" (11:4), so that he followed Astarte, Milcom, Chemosh, and Molech, to name a few, building shrines to them on "the hill east of Jerusalem" (11:7). What the kings of those nations could not have done with their armies, Solomon himself brought to pass by his own edicts and with the wealth God had entrusted to him. So the man who built a temple that honored God and prayed at its dedication one of the most memorable prayers in the Scriptures chooses as an old man to totter from one pagan shrine to another, playing the fool! A poor, old fool. "The Lord had commanded Solomon about this very thing, that he shouldn't follow other gods. But Solomon didn't do what the Lord commanded" (11:10).

What made him do it? How could this man of wisdom stumble into such foolishness? I'm sure flattery played a part. The Queen of Sheba announced at the conclusion of her visit to Solomon that before coming she couldn't believe the stories she had heard about Solomon's greatness, but now she realized that "the half of it wasn't even told to me" (1 Kings

10:7). You'd have to be a tough self-critic now to congratu-late yourself after such eloquent praise.

It's clear that over the years Solomon forgot some very important things. He forgot that his role as king was a gift from God; there were siblings who had seniority. He forgot that God had endowed him with unique wisdom, the envy of the nations. He even forgot his own prayer, when at the ded-ication of the temple he had said that God was a covenant-keeper who blessed those who showed loyalty and "who walk before you with all their heart" (1 Kings 8:23 NRSV). It's sur-prising how easy it is to forget past spiritual experiences, including our past prayers. The great souls have a more sub-stantial memory. John Newton, the Anglican cleric who gave us the hymn, "Amazing Grace," wanted to be sure that nei-ther he nor future generations would ever forget the divine mercy he had experienced. In the epitaph he prepared for his own burial he wrote, "John Newton, Clerk, once an Infidel and Libertine . . . by the rich mercy of our Lord and Saviour Jesus Christ, preserved, restored, pardoned, and appointed to preach the faith he had long laboured to destroy." Solomon would have done well to have engraved his earlier prayer where he could read it in later, faltering days.

So how, with the passing of years, do we protect ourselves from unseemly foolishness? To begin with, we remember our past. Remember where we came from, the people who have blessed us by their words, their gifts, and their love, the times we have been saved from our own sins and foolishness. We remember how many unearned blessing have enriched our lives. It's no great tragedy to forget where we left our keys or some name or event, but it's quite another thing to forget past blessings—because the memory of whom we are and the nature of our indebtedness is character memory. And it's also good religion.

Also, we learn to listen to praise with healthy amusement. Don't show your amusement, because to do so may be an unkindness to those who praise you. But whisper to yourself some counter arguments against such praise, and smile in your soul.And keep biblically sound. Remember the royal mistakes of Israel's kings, great souls who erred when they should have known better. Remind yourself that the Bible includes such stories for our personal benefit.

Then we do well to lay alongside the Bible stories something of our own biographies. Travel through the memories that bless and the memories that burn. Give thanks for the goodness of God that has made you rich in so many ways, then give thanks for the sins of which you've been forgiven, the perils you've escaped, the mistakes from which you've recovered. A trip down such a memory lane does much to balance the soul when one is temporarily carried away by a flattering word or a bit of success.

And we need to learn how to recognize the warning signs that the Spirit of God faithfully raises in our own souls—some by way of conscience, some by way of friends or family, and some by old-fashioned common sense. By a certain age, we should know the nature of the highway on which we're traveling, know it well enough to protect ourselves against life's sharp curves and steep inclines. We should also know when our soul is running low on fuel.

Growing older is a lovely gift, but ironically it has its own hazards. Some old fools have demonstrated as much. God's grace and God's wisdom, however, are abundant for every age. And the older one grows, the better one realizes it, and unashamedly receives the gift.

CHAPTER 4

By All Means, Go Home Again

T homas Wolfe was one of the great novelists of the first half of the twentieth century, competing in a period of notable American writers. The title of one of Wolfe's novels (and one I have especially enjoyed) became a phrase in our common speech: "You can't go home again."

I think I know what Wolfe was trying to say, and from what I know of his life story I think I know why he said it. Nevertheless, I am inclined to argue with him. I not only think a person can go home again but also believe we ought to make it our business to do so. It is particularly important as the years go by. And if we have decided that we want not only to grow old, but to grow older, we especially ought to go home again.

All of us have roots somewhere. Those who grow up as children of military families or corporate employees may feel that they are virtually rootless, but it isn't so. Their roots may not have depth in a particular place, but they are roots nevertheless. While they may be more widespread and perhaps therefore not as individually strong, when you put them together the scattered roots are as strong and significant to the owner as the more contained and deeper roots are to the person who grew up in one place.

I grew up in one city for the first seventeen years of my life and only twice traveled more than a hundred miles away during all of those years. The years of my growing-up were rather simple years in a small world, a world that grew still smaller during the Great Depression, when travel became even more restricted for those of us who experienced the broken economy most directly. I loved my home town and the area surrounding it, but I didn't know how important it was to my soul until sometime in my late fifties or early sixties. Now I consider a year ill spent if I don't make a pilgrimage to Sioux City, Iowa.

I have no right to say how Thomas Wolfe might have felt about Asheville, North Carolina, if he had lived long enough to get an extended perspective on the place. Dying before he was forty robbed Wolfe of that privilege. Perhaps even at sixty he still might have insisted that you can't go home again. However, I like to think that if he could have gone home at a later point in his life he might have exorcised some of his personal demons and found that there were more angels in his paths than he had previously known. Some might argue that if he had done so, he wouldn't have written with such poignancy. Perhaps. But naming our demons and setting them in context need not make our human stories shallow or feel-good; rather the stories gain a holy complexity that is missing if we concentrate on one side of life to the exclusion of the others.

When folks ask me why I go back to Sioux City every year, since my immediate family is gone and very few of my high school classmates still live there (or anywhere else, come to think of it!), I explain that I return for two reasons—to give thanks and to repent. I give thanks, at length and by names and specific events for the blessings of my childhood and youth, and I repent that I have not made better use of the time and love that kind people invested in me. I repent, especially, that I never managed to thank some of those people. I didn't know how good they were or how much I owed them until I could no longer pay the debt.

So I go home again to consort with my ghosts. They're

almost all friendly ghosts. In fact I suspect that time has given benevolent faces to some who seemed otherwise at the time of our merged paths. Perhaps that's a foretaste of heaven, when we'll be able to see how some misfortunes and mistreatments later worked to good. In the biblical story Joseph was able to say to the brothers who had sold him into slavery, "You planned something bad for me, but God produced something good" (Genesis 50:20). So my ghosts are friendly ones, whether they wished it so or not.

I go to the places where I went to church and Sunday school; neither of the churches is now in that location. I go to the grade schools, junior high school, and high school, some of which are now empty lots and others converted to different usage. I go to the location of three public libraries, which rank just below churches, homes, and schools in my list of sacred places. And particularly, I go to the thirteen homes I can still locate from those years, though some are now empty lots. My parents were renters. My mother had a restless streak that made her think a different house would of course be better for some reason or other, and my father was a patient man who tried to please her. Except for our upright piano, our furniture was limited so moving was mostly manageable with my father's delivery truck and the help of my strong brothers-in-law.

All of these places are sacred to me. I recall names as I stand on a corner or sit on a nearby bench. Some names are always there, because their role in my life is so easy to

measure. In some instances these persons were direct partic-
ipants for only a year, or in the cases of some teachers only a
semester, yet something about their person got through to
me. On reflection I have come to realize that it was not so
much their particular person as it was the state of my own
soul or mind at that time. Probably some would have
touched me not at all at a different time or under different
circumstances. Other persons come to my mind only once in
half-a-dozen trips. If I had the skills of a novelist, I could
populate a series of novels and short stories with these persons I knew so long ago. It seems to me that my world was
populated with a movie-maker's catalog of characters wait-
ing to come to life. I'm grateful I grew up before the world of
electronic games, or I might never have known all of those
fascinating people.

I learned early that all humans are a mix of good and bad,
noble and evil; the difference is generally a nuance, though
some weigh wonderfully toward the saint side, while others
seemed well on the road to perdition. Several summers during my early teens I worked as a hopper on a laundry and dry
cleaning delivery truck. This job took me into disreputable
hotels, houses of prostitution, and gambling operations
where three or four locks were opened before I could gain
admittance. I learned early that there were human beings in
all of these places and that the differences were more a matter of degree than of kind. These experiences prepared my
soul to preach and to pastor. I won't tell you that I was never

judgmental, because we humans always find it easy to pass judgment on others, since such judgments help us to excuse ourselves. However, I'm very sure I gained lessons in compassion and empathy that otherwise I would never have known.

Essentially my only pictorial record of those first seventeen years is the high school annual from my senior year. Because so much of that period was during the Great Depression, I never had the money to have my picture taken for the school annual or to purchase an annual until my senior year. But the single volume adds materially to the experience of going home again. When I see those persons who autographed the book by writing, "I'll never forget you!"—and sometimes more emphatically, "I'll never forget you! Never!!" I wonder how many could have recalled me even two decades later. Friendship is a wonderful, erratic, unpredictable, and illogical affair, so that the persons who once seemed monumental slip into obscurity, while others grow in significance in later years, even if we never see them again. I'm not sure what this proves, except that we should treat every human being with care. All of us humans have a remarkable capacity for friendship. Perhaps it is true that some have more capacity than others. But it seems to me more likely that our capacity shows itself when we are in a situation or with the type of person that brings out the better part of our self. Going home again—that is, re-evaluating the friendships and persons of our past—can help us to a better understanding of our own person, and with it, a greater readiness and ability for understanding the people we've known. Or thought we had known.

I said earlier that many places are sacred to me. Their sacredness is related, of course, to the people who populated those places. But the places themselves have a power of their own, and sometimes it is their power that lends beauty or sadness to the people whose ghosts inhabit the place. Besides, the people are no longer there, and in some instances I can't reconstruct their face or form. However, the buildings remain, and even if the current use of the building has nothing to do with its significance in my own life, I can repopulate it for my own purposes.

During a recent December, Frank Bruni, columnist with *The New York Times*, recalled the two years he lived in Rome and the college years spent in Chapel Hill, North Carolina. He observed that what bothered him most was not the degree to which the places had changed, but rather "how much everything has no doubt stayed the same, coupled with the recognition that I didn't appreciate or really even examine it before. The sorrow lies there" (Frank Bruni, "Time, Distance and Clarity," *New York Times*, A29, December 12, 2011).

I feel Bruni's sorrow. This article reflects the regret most of us feel when we remember people who now hold a more significant place in memory than they did in life, because now we have the capacity to appreciate them. But in this respect, places are better than persons. I can thank only the ghosts of persons or think of them through the lovely doctrine of the communion of saints, but I can still practice my appreciation for places. In some instances I've done so in a monetary way. I haven't the resources to fund a building or a library, but I've sent unsolicited gifts to two libraries that are very nearly sacred to me. At another time, I gave a more substantial contribution for the preservation of my old high school. The buildings are not a sentient thing, but I am, so I express myself in my human capacity to places that are unable to grasp my love.

I have said in many sermons and in a book or two that gratitude is one of humanity's finer traits. I exercise it when I go home again. I walk the four blocks around Central High School, "the Castle on a Hill," now a building of apartments and thank God with each step for the friends I knew, the teachers who blessed me, and the benefits I am still receiving from the a cappella choir, the classes in public speaking with F. O. Racker, and Miss Wachter's typing classes (what would I have done without them all of these years). I smile now that I couldn't survive even the first cut of the football and basketball tryouts, but it's just as well! I remember a teacher, though not by name, who convinced me that American history was dull, and I thank God for a university professor a decade later who gave me a love for the subject that has blessed the rest of my life. I remember how financially poor I was and how rich in friendships.

The city razed West Junior High School some years ago. I'm glad I wasn't there when it happened, or I might have set up a mourning spot in the way of the demolition crew. Now I go back to an empty lot, but the teachers are still there in my soul. I repopulate the auditorium with a procession of students and the memories of the thrice-weekly assembly programs that made life uniquely lively for a boy whose only other entertainment was the marvel of radio, pick-up games of softball, and the variety of evangelists who came to several churches in the city, often with what seemed to me to be marvelous musicians. I especially remember the great Billy Sunday, and a few years later, the young girl evangelist, Uldine Utley. They were, indeed, giants in the land in those days—because, of course, giants get their prominence partly by comparison with one's own height. Gulliver, after all, wasn't a giant until he came to the world of the Lilliputians.

I am so rich, so very rich, when I go home again.

I have spoken of my friendly ghosts. Some of you wish you could set me straight about these ghosts or offer some sort of rebuttal from your own quite different experience. I have no right to argue with you because I haven't walked in your shoes, nor do I have your feet. I know, too, that some of us have a tendency to glamorize persons from the past, just as memory makes a muddy wading pool into a lustrous lake. I know that my mother was inclined to be a hypochondriac and that my father was no doubt what today's counselors would call an enabler. Although they were earnest Christians and loyal church members, they were often critical of their ministers. I hope not many of my parishioners were as critical of me as my parents were of their pastors.

One of the ways to grow older without growing old is to become a beneficiary of your past rather than its victim or its prisoner. If our past fences us in with resentment and with desires for revenge, we are old before our time because the past holds us captive. If I can't forgive someone who has hurt me in the past, even if the hurting was mean and intentional, I am letting them control me years later. It is enough that someone hurt me when I was five or fifteen or fifty. Why let them continue to hurt me today? Why should I allow their deeds to control me still, decades later? A fine friend of years gone by, Clarke Hoak, loved to quote this wisdom: "If you fool me once, shame on you; if you fool me twice, shame on me." I extend that simple wisdom to those who seem to have done me wrong in the past. If they hurt me once, shame on them. If I allow them, through memory and resentment, to continue hurting me years later, shame on me.

Each time I go home again I try also to forgive myself. This is harder for me partly because I want to improve on myself and want to become better than I was. But as I talk with my ghosts of days long past and feel sad that I was unwise, ungrateful, or insensitive, I try to remember what my limitations were in those days. Gratitude, for example, is in some measure a learned trait. The infant that cries for food will emit sounds of pleasure when the food arrives by breast or bottle, but I doubt that gratitude is involved, just satisfaction and perhaps the feeling, "Why the long delay?" Later we learn, if indeed we mature, that we're fortunate when a table is spread before us, whether in the presence of friends or enemies. I'm sorry for the people I didn't always thank and those I'm sure I didn't thank adequately. How could I? How could I know I would still be quoting that person sixty years later or I would still be benefiting after that person's body had, in truth, returned to the dust from whence it came?

Some of us need to be as sympathetic and understanding of our own failures of the past as we seek now to be understanding of others. We need to remember that we were a work in progress then—as we are still, I hope—and that we had our unique problems and shortcomings that made it difficult for us to be as fine as we wish now we had been. It isn't fair to impose a sixty-year-old's judgment on a twelve-year-old's frame.

The sum of it all? Go home again! By all means, go home again! Thank God for the good people you once knew, and extend forgiveness in your own soul to those who once hurt you. Probably they weren't any wiser then than you were, so it's foolish to hold long-ago failures against them. Forgive the bullies; they must have had shortcomings aplenty to drive them to bullying, so they're more to be pitied than censured. Rejoice in all the good you can remember: good people, good places, good fun, good learning. And see what you can convert of the things that once seemed so bad. Embrace the best of your past, and convert the rest of it by the superior wisdom you now possess.

After all, you're growing older.

CHAPTER 5

—————

GROW OLD ALONG
WITH ME

Grow old along with me!" Robert Browning wrote it in "Rabbi Ben Ezra," and his attitude was just right, because he continued, "The best is yet to be, / The last of life, for which the first was made." I've heard some criticize Browning for his cheerful call to growing old, in light of his being only fifty-two at the time of his writing. I submit, however, that fifty-two was older by a good piece in the actuarial tables of 1864 than it is today. And come to think of it, even in our time the American Association of Retired Persons solicits your membership when you hit fifty.

I contend without the shadow of a doubt that Browning was right in his optimism, right philosophically in looking to the future with excitement rather than dread, and right in fact in insisting that these latter years are "The last of life, for which the first were made." Some unknown wise soul has said, "One of the gifts of getting older is that we get to keep all the ages we've been." This is a fine fact and one to remember. I sometimes dare to say to someone twenty or forty or sixty years younger, "I've been your age, but you've never been mine. I may not know your age in the context in which you know it, but the basic similarities are close enough that I have at least a fair notion of where you are. But you haven't the foggiest notion (beyond perhaps a sociological study) of where I am." This doesn't particularly impress many of those who are younger, but their inability to admit the point only demonstrates again how fine it is to grow older.

But what I want most to discuss just now is the opening line of Browning's poem: "Grow old along with me." That is, the special beauty of growing old with others, and the particular privilege of friendship as we grow older.

Before we go further let me say that I know something of the dark side of Browning's words, the point the poem doesn't mention in those bright opening lines. In the nearly forty years that I was a pastor, so often someone in a nursing home or a retirement community said, "It's very lonely when you're old, when there's no one who remembers you or who remembers what life was like when you were younger."

They have a point. I know it at first hand. I'm ready at even the hint of an invitation to tell about life during the Great Depression, but I find that my audience is diminishing steadily. Those who have some measure of interest are passing from the scene, and those in a younger generation have other interests, such as the newest improvement to their electronic device, or a new made-from-nothing public personality who interests me no more than the Great Depression interests my younger friend.

One of my best friends, though I never had a chance to meet him in the flesh, is Samuel Johnson (1709–1784). He was philosophical about the passing years, but his pain still slips through. It is the course of nature, he observed, that those who live long outlive those whom he loves and honors.[1] It's a gift to live long, especially if we're able to retain a reasonable measure of our physical and mental powers; yet with each passing year the circle of contemporaries grows smaller. John Donne was broadly right when he declared that every man's death diminished him.[2] From the point of view of one's emotional supports, we especially and dramatically are diminished when the death is from the circle of those who have known us best and longest, and who understand the world of our cherished memories.

Of course we want someone to grow old with us as we grow older. A great Scottish preacher of another day, Arthur John Gossip, reminded his congregation that "we are all the natives of a very small province of time. And the moment that we cross its borders into another generation, we find ourselves home-sick aliens in a strange land."[3] How strange? Gossip stays with his figure of speech: we discover that in this new land of another generation we find that we "always speak . . . with a palpably foreign accent."[4] If this was the experience many years ago, I venture that the generational accent is more pronounced many times today, with the accelerated pace of the electronic world and our current ability to enshrine an enthusiasm one day and bury it the next.

So is there any hope that we might find friendships to replace those that relocation or death take from us? Many contend from experience and observation that the best years for forming lifelong friendships are the period of high school and college years. Their definition of *lifelong* is not simply the length of friendship, for obviously a friendship can't be lifelong if it begins when one is fifty or sixty years of age. By "lifelong" we mean a certain emotional, empathetic quality, often related to the raw material of our psyche in our younger years.

I hold to a different view. We are most open to depth of friendship when we are most ready to allow someone to enter into our lives with depth; that is, at a time when we're willing to be vulnerable. We become more cautious and self-protective at a certain point—perhaps especially in our career-building years, when we're more fearful that if we reveal too much of ourselves we may suffer for it later. This may explain in a measure how it is that strangers on an airplane reveal things about themselves they would never tell to a co-worker or a fellow church member. They don't expect to see this seatmate again, so there's no danger in telling something that needs to be said so much to a fellow human being, but a safe one.

In some respects we may be more capable of true friendship in our later years than at any time since our kindergarten days. Children slip into friendships rather easily because they accept life at its fundamentals, which is what they know of life. In adult life, unfortunately, friendship can slip from these fundamentals because our culture encourages us to build relationships on what may be peripheral rather than on what is fundamental. Thus we form our ties on business or professional relationships or on political or social interactions. This is natural and reasonable, and I don't mean to treat it as evil. All of us know what it is, however, to meet an old work associate ten years later to discover that after we have reminisced about a few fellow co-workers and some humorous stories from the good old days, we have nothing more to say. I repeat, I don't mean to disparage such relationships; they have their place, and it is a deserving one. But such friendships are rarely the stuff of which profound ties are made.

Some of us get reconnected with old friends in later years. One of my classmates met a woman at his fiftieth class reunion whom he had known only incidentally in their high school days. Both were now widowed, and as they chatted they discovered that they had much in common; more, in fact, than was ever true in their teenage years. In time they married, to their mutual joy.

We never outgrow our need for friends. Indeed many older people will tell you that the need for friendship increases with the passing of time. Of course! Because if we become less able to travel, or we no longer have a career to occupy our time and attention, we have more time for what is the best of us, our relational capacity We may discover that we have allowed this part of our person to be neglected. We also may realize that we're now ready for a deeper kind of friendship. Whereas once we formed friendships on the basis of allies for a common cause or as someone who might help us in our career, now the friendship is on the simple but quite sound basis of simply liking one another. And not incidentally, it's quite possible that in growing older we have become more generous in our taste, so that we don't allow some superficial or transient details of a person to get in the way of friendship. That is, we've grown smart enough not to demand perfection in others which we aren't able to replicate in ourselves.

If we want to enlarge our circle of friendship in later years, what should we look for? We would do well to begin with some tough logic: Don't expect too much. At every age, friendship comes in different forms. There are those friends who are great for a cup of coffee or a glass of iced tea once every few weeks, but no more. In recognizing this fact we are passing no more of a judgment on this person than we are on ourselves. We shouldn't expect every person to become a deep, Jonathan-and-David type friend as shown in First Samuel. Some people are at their best for joining in watching a football game together, others for a unit of *Downton Abbey*. Some you enjoy sitting with in church or commiserating with at a committee meeting. And some, God bless them, will grow ten feet tall the day you are in a very hard place.

Generally speaking, there's much to be said for having some friends who make you laugh. A similar sense of humor is a delightful bond. When I speak of someone who makes you laugh, I don't necessarily mean a joke-teller. Not many people can tell a joke well. Fewer, as you know, than engage in the practice. Laughter is a way of looking at life, at knowing enough about yourself and other people to know that there are more reasons to laugh than to cry. Laughter is, indeed, good for the soul. Someone whose person makes you laugh will add, literally, months or years to your life—and at the same time, add fun to your years.

I cherish for you, as I cherish for myself, those friends who make me think. I'm not speaking about the person who loves to relate at length what they've just read or heard; I understand if you flee them like the plague. I'm speaking of those people who in routine conversation come up with an insight that sheds new light on the routine and which inspires you, in turn, to a thought that had never occurred to you before. One of the best signs of a thinking friend is that he makes you a better thinker. Good thinkers quicken the minds of the people around them. They don't necessarily direct the conversation by asking questions, but they invigorate talk by their own thoughts and by their appreciation for yours

That is, a good friend is almost surely a good listener. They care about you and the matters that concern you, and when they ask you a question it isn't a social formality. They really want to know how you are, what is happening with your children, or whether yesterday was a good day. The apostle Paul concluded his monumental theological discussions in the Book of Romans with all sorts of down-to-earth advice about living the Christian life. I like this word: "Be happy with those who are happy, and cry with those who are crying" (Romans 12:15). I turn again to my wise friend, Samuel Johnson: "But what is success to him that has none to enjoy it. Happiness is not found in self-contemplation, it is perceived only when it is reflected from another."[5] One of the loneliest moments in life is the occasion when something quite lovely or wonderful has happened to you, and you have no one who knows you well enough to know how much it means to you.

And a good friend—indeed, a great one—makes you strive. I thank God for friends who have made me want to be better than I am. It is not often by their preachments; people who exhort us often exhaust us. Those who inspire us to strive do so by their person and the light that comes from them. Leaving them you want to read something better, think something higher, and to love the best and flee not only from that which is base but also from what is mediocre.

Good friends also make you enjoy. It is not simply that you enjoy their company but that you enjoy other things more because you are in their company. Conrad Aiken put it into poetry: "Music I heard with you was more than music, / And bread I broke with you was more than bread."⁶ By their appreciation of what is good and beautiful, whether a biscuit, a ball game, or a prayer, your enjoyment is enhanced. They are generous enough to invite you into a place of enjoyment but wise enough not to compel you to enter, because each person's enjoyment is singularly defined.

And of course a good friend helps you to hope. Again, it is by example and contagion rather than by insisting or exhorting. Hope drives us on, not only to live another day but to bring glad expectation to the day. Hope keeps us marching around our Jericho until one day with a shout, we bring down its walls. This friend walks with us, reassuring us by his or her presence that life is worth the walk. She doesn't just tell us to smell the flowers, because being told only adds to our sense of failure; she smells the flowers and her obvious delight makes me smell them, too.

I hasten to say that my little list doesn't bring together all of the qualities you should look for. Tomorrow I might add to the list, and you surely will because your pilgrimage has contoured different lines for friendship. Also, especially, don't look for someone who fulfills all of these descriptions. This is too heavy an assignment for one person, and if you found such a person you would be in danger of destroying the combination by your consuming embrace. Appreciate and enjoy whatever friends you find and whatever particular roles they fill. Between them you may have a montage of friendship. And of course (and it's the "of course" that we're likely to forget): to have such friends we must be such friends; not miracle workers, not possessed of all virtue, but unselfish enough to be the kind of person that you want others to be.

So what if the circle of friends is by attrition, growing smaller? Who, then, will grow old along with me? Can we still make friends as we grow older? Well, to return to this basic theme of this book, the chances are good as we grow older, but they're quite dim if we insist on growing old. If we are set in stone, unwilling to make room in our lives for that which is new or those who are different, there's not much chance of finding friends with whom to grow older. If in our search for friends we're looking for rather full replicas of the friend who has died, moved away, or somehow dropped out of our life, we'll probably not find friends as we grow older, we'll have to take the risk.

But if you'll recall, taking risks has always been the price of friend-making. Friendships rarely begin with a guarantee. In fact, I would be skeptical of one if it began with such an offer. You take a risk when you venture into the possibility of a friendship. Not because the other person intends to betray you or exploit you, though either one is a possibility, but simply because the other person is taking as much of a risk with you as you are with him or her. Friendship doesn't have to ring with eternity to be worth having. Most of us can remember a day in kindergarten or first grade when we went home with tears in our eyes because the person we thought would be our very special friend chose to give their playground or lunch time to someone else. The same disappointment is possible at forty, sixty, or eighty-five. Some people call it chemistry, which means that they don't understand it either. Try again tomorrow.

Don't rule out the possibility of friendship across the boundaries of age. It's true, as I noted earlier, that different generations speak not only with a different accent but also in different languages. But that doesn't mean that we can't find areas of exciting agreement. Indeed, this may be the secret, that you will talk about more simple, more profound, and more deeply real things just because you have no common ground on what may be quite superficial matters.

Come to think of it, there's something to be said for finding a younger friend or two. It's a little like finding a doctor who's young enough that he or she won't retire before you exit: The younger friend is likely to be around. And don't rule out a person whose tastes are quite different. Opposites don't attract as often when we're older as when we were younger, but sometimes the challenge is still good for us.

One word more. I don't mean to transfer the burden to God, but pray about this friendship thing. God is the author of friendship and the Bible overflows with friendship stories at all levels and between vast varieties of people. Some theologians remind us that the Trinity itself is the essence of friendship. We should take hope in this truth, while remembering that our human friendships are limited by the fact that both parties are imperfect. But do know that God cares about your friendships and your justified need to have someone to grow older with. Such friendships will insure that the best is yet to be. Perhaps, in fact, the friendship for which all those earlier friendships were preparing you.

CHAPTER 6

If All Those Endearing Young Charms

Thomas Moore, the Irish poet from the first half of the nineteenth century, had a gift not only for putting words together in memorable fashion but also for being an able composer. When he tied his poetry to a fitting melody, there was twice the chance that what he wrote would stay in people's memory. Even so, I doubt that many these days recognize the words I've chosen for the title of this chapter. It's not only that we move faster physically via automobile and plane, our tastes move more rapidly, too, sometimes one gets the impression that nothing is good unless it is recent. I wonder if we will come to a time when we'll label our music or books like our cereal and dairy products: "Not recommended for use after the following date." As for Thomas Moore, the lyrics and melody I have in mind are now nearly two centuries old, so I have no right to think they might be familiar to you. Besides, the lyrics are sentimental, which quickly disqualifies them in the minds of some.

So I won't quote the whole poem, "Believe Me, If All Those Endearing Young Charms." Moore wants his beloved to know that if charms he sees today were to disappear tomorrow, nothing in his love would change. Indeed, "around the dear ruin each wish of my heart / Would entwine itself verdantly still." But even if forgotten now, no doubt in the past roughly two centuries literally millions of persons throughout the English speaking world, and probably millions more in several translations, have made such a vow or have wished that their partner would do so.

Ironically, our devotion to "all those endearing young charms" is greater than it has ever been. But now the devotion is not necessarily to the presence of those charms in the person we love; rather, it seems increasingly that our special concern is with the charms, if I may call them that, which we see each morning when we look in the mirror. Or more likely, the charms we see in the mirror when we're about to head to work or to a social occasion. We live now in the world of the forever young. More correctly, we exist in the world of forever appearing young, or of seeking to look young. We don't mind receiving retirement benefits if only we can collect them without a wrinkle.

I hasten to say that I am in no way opposed to looking nice. I love looking at that which is beautiful, whether a painting, a tree, or a human being. And I have some sympathy with the issue of age when strangers or casual acquaintances ask, "Say, how old are you?" The question probably ranks on the social scale along with, "How much do you weigh?" or "What was your income last year?" If the biblical wise man was right when he said, "Gray hair is a crown of glory; / it is found on the path of righteousness" (Proverbs 16:31), why would one want to look like someone fresh out of college? If our tastes ever catch up with the Book of Proverbs, the market for hair coloring will be turned upside down.

But don't rush to buy stock in such a possibility. The market for looking young promises to be with us for a long while. There will be a few individuals who are so at peace with the face and form they've gotten or so vigorously independent of contemporary judgments that no promise of a youth treatment will attract them. But I suspect they will remain a minority. Meanwhile cosmetology and plastic surgery will rule the day.

One has a feeling that any personality in the entertainment world who has refused plastic surgery is seen as a marvel, a freak, or a fraud, and the mood of Hollywood and New York has found its way into virtually every corner of America and Canada. According to The American Society for Aesthetic Plastic Surgery, in 2007, there were nearly twelve million cosmetic procedures in the United States. There's room for all fifty states in that figure. And lest you think that this fascination with physical glamour is exclusively American, Europe is the second largest market for such surgery, investing over two billion dollars a year. And I don't want these statistics to mislead; not all of these cosmetic procedures have to do with age. A very great many are performed for some who are young but who have felt since pre-school that their ears were too protrusive or their nose uncute, and there are many of the young or middle aged who conclude that their only chance to win the battle of the bulge is to remove what has become the enemy.

My interest at this moment in our discussion is the process of aging and what aging does to our physical appearance. And I want to reaffirm that I have nothing against beauty; I'm all for it—though I want to be sure that its definition is not too small or cheap. Ultimately, in fact, I want to make a full-court press for beauty: the beauty that lasts because it is born from within rather than imposed from the outside.

Have you noticed as you read your Bible how little is said about physical appearances in general and physical beauty in particular? Genesis tells us nothing about the physical appearance of Adam and Eve except : "The two of them were naked, the man and his wife, but they weren't embarrassed" (Genesis 2:25). No doubt someone reading this wants to reply, "You see—they were lucky. They didn't need liposuction!" I doubt that this is what the writer of Genesis had in mind. We don't know anything about the physical appearance of Noah, Abraham, or Moses. And although Samson was strong beyond imagining, there's no measure of his abs. We know Goliath's height when he stepped into the ring against David, but all we know about David is that he was "reddish-brown, had beautiful eyes, and was good-looking" when the prophet Samuel found him (1 Samuel 16:12). But God had warned Samuel earlier that in seeking Israel's new king he should have "no regard for his appearance or stature" (16:7).

The New Testament is even sparser in its descriptions of its characters. I venture that more artists over more centuries have painted Mary, the mother of Jesus, than any other woman in history or legend, yet we know absolutely nothing about her appearance. So, too, with the apostle Paul, though he dares to mention that the people who heard him preach said "in person he is weak and his speech is worth nothing" (2 Corinthians 10:10). As for Jesus, although the four Gospels are dedicated to his story, and follow him from before conception until his resurrection and ascension, they tell us nothing, absolutely nothing, about his physical appearance. No wonder artists in every culture have made Jesus their own, beginning with the Europeans and continuing today into the world's developing nations. We know a very great deal about our Lord, about his character, his ministry, his suffering and death, and his place in the godhead, but nothing about his physical appearance.

So what shall we say about growing older, and the effects of aging on our physical bodies and our general physical appearance? What about the sagging that tends to come with age unless we fight constantly against it, or turn to the surgeon to counter it? What about the wrinkles that come to face or hands or more hidden parts of our anatomy? And what of the changes in our complexion, including the beauty spots of age? And hair! Not so long ago the barber used thinning shears to keep the hair manageable, and now the barber's successor, by whatever name, talks more and cuts less in order to fill the time allotted to your presence. We understand that some joints are going to show signs of wear and that sight or hearing may need assistance or even surgery. But with it all, is it necessary that we *look* old?

Obviously, with the aid of cosmetic surgery or aesthetic surgery, we can make a difference. If you choose to do so it is quite clearly your business and not mine, and probably my right to an opinion is at the same level as my feelings about your scarf, blouse, sweater, or necktie: if what you wear or what you do to your body or face seems appropriate to your person and your budget, bravo.

But I would like to offer a word on behalf of the enduring older charms. That is, I don't think that you and I are nature's finished product the day we're born. In fact, I ponder often how it is that we take so many pictures of infants. In this new generation of easy photography, we often take literally hundreds of photos of them. In truth their features have little to distinguish them from all the rest of their kind, much as we doting parents and grandparents want to think otherwise. And we take so few pictures in later years when we're getting a face of our own.

Someone has said that in our mid to late teens we humans have the face God has given us, but beginning in our twenties we gradually get the face we've earned. I agree fully with Roger Rosenblatt when he writes, "The only way a young woman can really be beautiful is when some element of difference, of strangeness, is present alongside her perfect, unblemished features" ("Secret Admirer," *Modern Maturity* [August–September 1993]: 29). If one wants a world where everyone looks alike, it would have to be the product of an unmercifully scientific age, something out of Aldous Huxley in *Brave New World*. But this would be a world of automatons, not of human beings.

Because to be human is to be in a constant state of growth, and of course growth means change. To be human is to once have been an infant, then a teenager, then an adult; and to be an adult means an almost ceaseless series of personality-shaping and thus form-shaping events. If I were a painter tracing John Bunyan's literary character Christian in *The Pilgrim's Progress*, I would portray awesome, though sometimes subtle, changes in his face. At first he would look like any mortal. We'd probably want him to be handsome, by whatever our definition of the word, with a steady gaze and an interesting face. But the face can't be too interesting at the outset of his pilgrimage because he hasn't experienced enough to get those exquisite contours. What's interesting in his face is what he has inherited from his ancestors. He doesn't yet have many features that are really his own.

But watch what happens as the pilgrim passes through the Slough of Despond. Stay there for a while and it will leave its mark on your face as well as your mind. And pity the pilgrim as he struggles on the Hill Difficulty. Vanity Fair may sound quite enchanting, but believe me it leaves its imprint on the face as well as on the soul. And Doubting Castle! Stay there long enough and even the hardiest pilgrim will have some deeply-etched lines around the eyes and lips.

A very sensitive artist could trace Pilgrim's journey in a series of paintings, but I venture that many of the changes would be subtle enough that only a very attentive observer would catch them all. The finished portrait, I declare, would rightly be titled, "The Pilgrim as Saint," and he'd have the marks to show it. I once had a neighbor who had been a catcher in major league baseball. I thought sometimes as I looked at his hands that he could date some of his career by the joints in his fingers and thumbs and the scars repairing them. Pilgrim's face would look like that; and I dare to declare that not only would his face tell a story—his spiritual biography—but that it would be beautiful. There would be none other quite like it.

This is as it should be. We note often that each person has unique fingerprints and footprints. The life we live proceeds to give us a face, and it is uniquely ours; because our unfolding persons are products not only of our experiences but also of the way we respond to those experiences. People emerge from a natural disaster with feelings as different as profound hopelessness to an exhilarating sense of challenge, with variations between at a multitude of levels. In time those reactions take shape on face and neck, hands and soul.

But hear me. What we experience of good and ill, and whatever the fortune that life seems to send our way, by health or sickness, abundance or limitation, victories or defeats, these matters are only a small part of the shaping of the face. What we think does more to determine the contours of our person than what we experience. Health specialists tell us, correctly, that we are what we eat. It is even truer that we are what we think. We may tell ourselves that no one knows what we're thinking but you can't fool a soul forever, and eventually what we think will come out, in some form or other, in the face.

In a long lifetime of speaking in thousands of public occasions, mostly religious but a great many secular, I have studied hundreds of thousands of faces. I look at the people to whom I am speaking; that's how I learn who they are and what they're saying to me. Some faces make me despairing of the human race, because they seem artificial, or bored with life, or possessed by deep selfishness and unhappiness. Other faces give me hope. They are living life as honestly and as deeply as they can, and they are winning.

But every face is a work in progress. And it is steadily becoming what we're making it. We can't prevent some of the natural aging of skin and hair, though with proper attention to rules of health and diet we can delay the process. And we can play a major part in what goes into our brain and how long we let it stay there. We can become hospitable to that which edifies and resistant to that which depresses, irritates, or corrupts. It's often difficult to control our feelings, but we can go a long way toward controlling our attitudes, and if our attitude is healthy it will cut back on potentially destructive feelings.

All of us would like to be physically attractive as we grow older. We should do everything in our power to make it so, by care and taste in the way we dress and by watching our weight, our posture, and our general grooming. But in the long run an extraordinary amount of our physical attractiveness—especially in our face—is a product of what we are inside. Now and again I see people both young and old who have spent a good deal on clothing and general grooming and perhaps on cosmetic remaking, too, but have forgotten a major wardrobe item. They've forgotten a smile. But of course this isn't surprising, because a true smile is a long-term investment. It's no wonder therefore that people spend their money on clothes and exterior factors instead, because one can buy these within an hour or two, or a few weeks longer if a surgical procedure is used. Meanwhile a good smile has to do with one's attitude toward the human race and toward God.

In the course of thinking about this subject, I read some advertisements for aesthetic surgery. "Revitalize your image," one said. And another, "Envision a new you." In turn, I began thinking how a church might advertise itself. "Look sharp! Read the Book of Proverbs." Or "To get a youthful smile, try being born again!" Or perhaps, "Learn from Moses how to be at your best at 120." And again, "Want to be glamorous after you're 65? Learn from Abraham's wife, Sarah."

I'm just kidding, and I hope I don't see one of those lines in a church bulletin board. But I'm serious about "those endearing young charms" when we give God a chance to grow them into those endearing and enduring older charms. It's better to start young, but miracles are possible at any age. I believe a smile can be born again at age eighty, and that when this happens the smile has far more content and true winsomeness than even a teenager's best grin.

Roger Rosenblatt said, "It is not an easy thing to age beautifully. It has to do with aging happily, and that, I think, has to do with continuing to see the world as an adventure" ("Secret Admirer"). I agree. I think that's the point with John Bunyan's story of the pilgrim: for him, life with Christ was an adventure. That's probably also why we call his story *The Pilgrim's Progress*, emphasis on the words progress. I insist that he was a better looking person when he died than he was at fifteen. Charm, indeed!

CHAPTER 7

THERE IS MUCH LAND
YET TO BE POSSESSED

In a sense everything about this book is personal for both you and me. Since I'm writing about age from the vantage point of my own age, not only do I make personal references but also everything about the subject is woven through the warp and woof of my soul. And it's personal for you because almost everything I'm writing about is meant to be used in a personal way. At times I feel that I'm in danger of being intrusive, and at other times it's almost as if we're sitting together in a living room or backyard, talking. On some occasions I half expect you to interrupt me.But this particular chapter is *especially* personal—partly because of the way the theme came to me and partly because the place of supreme importance that the convictions of this chapter hold in my own life.

Sometime in the early spring of 2004 I underlined a verse in the course of my early morning Bible reading. This wasn't unusual for me; if a book is mine, it either gets underlined and bracketed, or it gets laid aside and eventually discarded. I was reading a translation of the Bible that was new to me so I was enjoying the particular excitement of fresh, clean pages and frequent new insights. But I confess that I wasn't especially hopeful at this point in my reading because I was in the Old Testament Book of Joshua, and Joshua is not one of my favorite books. I understand why all the war and bloodshed are there, but I don't like it.

Nevertheless, it was in Joshua that I came upon this special verse. I underlined it, but that wasn't enough; I copied it down, and with special care. And I didn't copy it on a file card or a piece of stationery, I copied it on the facing page of the back cover of my *Daily Suggester*, a little black date book that I've gotten annually from The United Methodist Publishing House since the early 1950s.

I had never before copied a verse in my pocket *Suggester*.

Indeed, I've always been a bit discomfited when someone has asked me to name my favorite Bible verse, because I don't have a favorite. I have hundreds of favorites, but not a single favorite to put on my tombstone or to write under my signature like some better preachers and theologians do. But this verse was different. I knew it was mine. Here it is:

> You are old and advanced in years and there remains yet
> very much land to possess. (Joshua 13:1 ESV)

This was God's special message to Joshua, Moses' successor. Joshua's assignment had been to take the land of Canaan by military conquest. He had worked hard and effectively at his task but now he was "old and advanced in years," and the job was still far from done.

I have identified myself as a Christian since I was ten years old and God has blessed me in more ways than (obviously) I have deserved. But in all of my long Christian life, I haven't had many experiences that one might call mystical. And for that matter, this verse didn't light up on the page as I read it, and I didn't hear any voices. No matter; I knew it was mine, and I celebrated the fact by recording it in the little book that is in my pocket every waking hour, in a place where I could remind myself that God had given me a word. Each year since that spring day in 2004, when I open a new *Daily Suggester* and begin entering dates, addresses and telephone numbers for the coming year, I write this verse in its demanding place, in the facing page of the inside back cover.

Part of the verse was no surprise. I knew I was old and advanced in years because the calendar told me so, and my body indicated in several ways that the calendar was right. But I didn't know what land—"very much" at that—remained to be possessed. As it happens, a few months later the administration at Asbury Theological Seminary asked me to serve for a year as a Dean. That was a "land" I had never known before, but I accepted the call and as it turned out, served two years before a permanent appointment was made. After that, a still more unlikely call came, this time to serve as president of the Seminary during a very difficult period of transition. This was new land for sure, and like the Israelites of old, I found that there were giants in the land. I carried these responsibilities for nearly three years before the seminary's trustees found a longer term appointee for the presidential office.

These extraordinary assignments at a point so late in one's life would seem like a rather clear fulfillment of the verse that was now in my pocket guide. I knew better, however. I had sensed almost from the beginning that the "very much land" that awaited me was not career or travel or unexpected honors. It was the most important unconquered land imaginable: the land of my own soul. In the classic language of the King James Version, "He that is slow to anger is better than the mighty; and he that ruleth his spirit than he that taketh a city" (Proverbs 16:32). Military experts have proved ten thousand times over that with several years of good training and experience a commander can take a city. But most of us have found that it takes a long lifetime to rule one's own spirit, and some of us wonder if even a lifetime will suffice.

So I'm now on the quest of the saints: I want to be a truly good human being. In biblical language, I want to become Christ-like. Let me recast our Lord's words: "What shall it profit a person if he or she succeeds in work and community, is financially secure, is generally well-thought-of, and is physically healthy, but never becomes the person God wanted him to be?"

Doesn't God want more for us than a good investment portfolio? I'm glad for my diplomas and some academic awards along the way, but do you think they will impress our Lord? Jesus told a parable about the final judgment, with some going to eternal punishment and others going to eternal life (Matthew 25:31-46), but there's nothing there about the things we often prize, like athletic awards, election to office, recognition by notable people, or the size of our portfolio.

Of course I started young in my campaign to conquer this promised land of my own soul, but now I'm heaven-bent for winning. John Killinger tells a story for which he can't identify the source. A grandfather is spending a beautiful day with his young grandson, fishing and talking. The boy is at the full-of-questions age, and he plies his grandfather with them, one after another. Near the end of the day, as they've begun to pack up for their return home, the boy asks, "Grandpa, does anybody ever see God?" The grandfather is slow to answer. He weighs his thoughts and then his words, then answers with a report on his own soul. "Son, it's getting so I hardly see anything else."

You and I automatically don't become more spiritual as we grow older, but the odds are strong that we will give more time and attention to God. A survey by the Pew Research Center in 2009 measured the percentage of persons who say religion is very important in their life. Forty-four percent said so in the 18 to 29 age group, and 61 percent of those 50 to 64, but an impressive 70 percent for those ages 75 and over. I have quoted the great Samuel Johnson earlier. On Easter Eve in 1779 he wrote in his journal, "Of resolutions I have made so many, with so little effect, that I am almost weary, but, by the help of God, am not yet hopeless. . . . I am almost seventy years old, and have no time to lose." I am older than Johnson was when he wrote those words, and I understand the feeling. There is so much land yet to be taken, and each day I have less time to make the conquest.

So what am I doing about it, and what do I recommend to you? I'm satisfied that you, too, know that there is more to life than getting and spending, more than keeping up with the fashions, and more than having a good time. Indeed, you've become wiser about the pursuit of good times, so that now when you seek a good time you generally have a better sense of where to find it and how to enjoy it. But time goes by, and one has less time and sometimes less energy to get life's benefits. What shall we do if we want the ultimate, a life that pleases God and that fulfills our own deepest intentions;

and that in truth leaves us most fulfilled and most deeply satisfied?

To begin with, we have to get intentional about this pursuit. The old phrase, "all roads lead to Rome," may be true, but you won't live long enough to get there unless you give serious attention to the map and to signs along the way. I don't think many saints know that they're saints (though others may have seen the signs), and, for that matter, I doubt that many saints set out to be just that. But I am sure that those who find true fullness in Christ have set their souls to that goal and they strive for it with singular intention and intensity. The apostle Paul called it his goal, and he makes clear that he has set his whole being toward reaching it (Philippians 3:12-14).

Before I go farther, let me assure you that it's not too late for you to begin. The fact that you're making a late start may add precious intensity to your effort. To use the language of your school days, you may go about this the way you once crammed for your exams: the nearer the hour of the showdown, the more focused your attention. Besides, our walk of faith makes use of all the prior stuff of our journey. This includes not only the holiness we have already found, but also our experiences with that which is stupid, inept, ugly, and even sinful. Saint Paul looked back on his earlier life and described it as "sewer trash" (Philippians 3:8), yet this was the stuff that God later put to use. Nothing in our past is useless when once we decide to give ourselves fully to our Lord and to set our minds completely on becoming what God wants us to be.

Believe me, the intention is crucial. Paul tells the people at Philippi about the intention that is driving him because it is uppermost in his mind. It is more than his guiding principle, it is his compelling life force. He knows where he intends to go. He confesses readily that he isn't yet there, but this hasn't discouraged him, and he won't allow his failure to distract him. He wants to reach the goal for which he feels Christ has gotten hold of him.

This should be a constant encouragement in our quest. Our Lord had something in mind in getting hold of us, and it wasn't for us to die in spiritual mediocrity. If true godliness is God's will for you and me, what greater incentive do we need, and what greater assurance of making it?

On the whole, while having grand expectations, set your pace by simple, attainable steps. Do you currently spend fifteen minutes a day in some kind of spiritual devotion? Raise it by ten minutes. (If you wonder where to find ten minutes, you'll find it at your internet, television or telephone.) Invest those ten extra minutes in some continuing reader that will enlarge your mind and soul, or add names to the list of persons for whom you will pray. Or make prayer part of some of your current activity—walking, driving, or exercising

Incorporate God's presence into the other business of your life. As you read or listen to the news, pray for the victims of fire or accident or violence rather than simply bemoaning the state of the world. Any thoughtless soul can moan about what's wrong; saints pray and work to make a difference. As you respond to email or its various equivalents, pray for those to whom you communicate or who have communicated with you. As you check your bank statement, examine your accounts not just for accuracy but also for quality: Is this the way my money should be spent if, in truth, my money has something to do with my relationship with God? (Believe me, it does.) In the times when you're forced to wait for some reason—a medical or legal appointment, a telephone call, a traffic light—pray. When we fret, we eat away the moments of our lives. When we pray, we turn those moments into the very stuff of eternity.

What we read, listen to, watch, and talk about plays a large part in our spiritual conquest. That is, *words* are crucial in the conquest of our souls because words play so big a part in our being human. Words give us the ability to shape our thoughts and feelings and to understand the thoughts and feelings of others. Thus words play a unique part in our walk with God, by way of what we read and hear. Seek reading material that lifts,challenges, or catches hold of your soul. Cherish those persons with whom conversation is at times a sacrament. The right words lift our souls to higher ground, sometimes by admonition but more often simply by their quality and appropriateness to where we are.

But spiritual progress is by no means measured simply by our spiritual pursuits. It is so much a part of our daily, hourly, momentary conduct. A person I know well chose on a recent Lenten season to give up impatience and critical judgment of other people. Obviously she hoped to make these changes permanent, but Lent was a good season to begin, and often some of the best things we do are more feasible if we set a time for them. If one can manage a conduct change for seven weeks, as in Lent, it's feasible that with care and attention the change can continue forever.

Lent can be somewhat like New Year's resolutions except that with Lent we've attached our goal to a high purpose and a sacred setting. But the odds are that you aren't reading this during Lent. In that case, make your own, particular Lenten period. Establish your own time table—seven weeks, a month, a week; or like an alcoholic, a day—and set yourself to take this period by conquest for God and your soul. If a quick temper has beset you all your life, go after it. If an unkind tongue too often asserts itself in your conversation, or an unkind thought, though unspoken, occupies too much space in your mind, go after it now, and set a time of being free from it. And obviously, seek God's help in this pursuit. If I understand the Holy Spirit correctly, God is even more concerned about your winning the battle in question than you are. Indeed, I submit that it is the Holy Spirit that has put the conquest idea into your mind.

Not long ago a magazine promised on its cover that one of its articles would show twenty-four hours to a longer life. I read and appreciated it. But I reminded myself from the beginning that a longer life is not of itself the promise we need. If you aren't enjoying the years you now have, what do you gain by adding more years of disappointment or unfulfillment? The best reason for many people to extend their years is the hope that perhaps in those years they might still find a *fuller* life. And that's what I'm proposing for you and for me: a life that is full.

Jesus said, "I came so that they could have life—indeed, so that they could live life to the fullest" (John 10:10). If this is God's purpose in sending Jesus Christ into the world, I dare to feel that God wants all of us to have such a life. And I move logically then to another conviction. If God wants us to have a full life, God must have particular interest in those who are older, because they have less time remaining to enjoy such fullness. And God knows that those who are older have now lived long enough (if they've learned anything at all) to have a better sense of what is worth going after.

So I'm here to tell you, whatever your age, that there is much land yet to be possessed, and it is located in our own souls. Ultimately, no achievement in life is more crucial, more significant, and more fulfilling than taking this land for God and for grand, holy, happy living. So put on the full armor of God and become one of God's happy warriors. Because this land of your soul is the land God wants most for you and me to conquer.

CHAPTER 8

REDEEM THE TIME

I don't know if the apostle Paul was the first to say it, but he said it most memorably. "See then that ye walk circumspectly, not as fools, but as wise, / Redeeming the time, because the days are evil" (Ephesians 5:15-16 KJV). Do you want to be wise? Redeem your time. Want to live like a fool? Spend your time without knowing where it's going.

Paul wrote in a world where people measured time by the

sun. He didn't know about split seconds, wrist watches, Greenwich mean time, or daylight saving time. But he knew that time is limited and that if you don't redeem it, time will go to waste. Further, he knew that "the days are evil," that every kind of destructive, sinful, unworthy and useless power is loose in our world, stealing our time from us. It is in our power, under God, to redeem our time. But it's up to us.

"Not in my case," someone quickly answers—someone who's working three jobs, or taking care of an infirm relative or friend, or someone whose life is often occupied by persons who seem oblivious to one's own needs or rights. Of course I don't know the specifics of your life, and I will not be so unwise as to reply, "We're all busy," because that statement is far too simple. Some of us have less control of our time than others. I want only to make us sensitive to the value of time in general so that we begin to work in specific ways to redeem the hours that come each day with our name written on them.

Let me begin with what may seem like a very heavy word and perhaps even a morbid one. I am almost certain it was in the background of Paul's thinking because Paul knew the Book of Psalms very well, very possibly by memory. Listen:

Let me know my end, LORD,
  How many days do I have left?
I want to know how brief my time is (Psalm 39:4).

Both Paul and David knew the value of time. They judged its value in light of their relationship to God.

Amy Bloom, the contemporary novelist, tells of a visit with an elderly friend who said, as she tapped her watch, "Look, darling: From age 50 to 80 it's not minutes, it's seconds. Pay attention." Not sure Miss Bloom was getting her point, the older woman continued, "It's seconds. You think you know, but you don't."[1]

And of course we don't. Perhaps we couldn't handle it if we did. Life, like the waters of the sea, needs an ebb and flow. But we need to think seriously enough about time to remember that time is, indeed, God's priceless gift, and that as Leon Danco has said, "Whatever successes we may achieve in this life will come from the purpose to which we put" this priceless gift.[2]

I believe that in one sense the persons whom we describe as being middle aged are probably the most sensitive about the value of time. The young often see time only as something to be hurried through until they get to one of its high points—driver's license, senior prom, college, commencement, marriage, career-type job—while the quite old think that the time left to them is something simply to enjoy, without undue attention to the clock. But I'm not at all sure that the middle period, when life is most under the control of the ticking clock, is necessarily when it is treated most rightly and sacredly. The inclination at the middle time of life is to see life as a commodity—"time is money," as the phrase goes—when in truth, if time is no more than money, it doesn't deserve particular attention. But if time is life itself, a gift from God, a piece of what our poor imaginations think eternity will be—well, then, time is sacred and should be touched with the awe, reverence, and care that we show to anything that we consider truly sacred.

Those who are growing older are in a favored position for realizing this and for living accordingly. They are old enough to know that time is not money (except, perhaps, when they're paying for surgery or medications to sustain it a bit longer). And on the other hand, it is not in unlimited supply, as the very young assume. I don't know how old the psalmist was when he anxiously pondered how many days he had left to live. Perhaps he was in what seemed the latter years of his life, or perhaps he was only forty but had a moment of premature wisdom. Poets are sometimes like that, as of course aging baseball players are.

But it is very good wisdom for those who are growing older. There is value, not morbidity, in getting a sense of our mortality. It's wise to realize that the actuarial tables are intruding on us. We may well outsmart the averages, but we know they're there, and it's good to know this. We need to realize that there is a conclusion to our earthly story because this introduces uncommon sense to our whole outlook on the wonder of life. It gives unique grandeur to each day. We come to know that there are no ordinary days. Each one is, indeed, crafted by God, and each is a holy gift.

So how should we redeem the time? How should we number our days? Robert Browning had an answer in "The Flight to the Dutchess": "What's a man's age? He must hurry more, that's all; / Cram in a day, what his youth took a year to hold." To be honest, I don't want to take Browning too literally. I've lived a "hurry" life and a "cram" life. What I want for you and for me is in a sense a more deliberate life; that is, one that we've deliberated upon so that we are choosing where our time is going rather than feeling at the end of the day (or worse, at the end of a year) that somehow the time was stolen from us when we weren't looking.

I want to examine where my time is going (it goes by seconds, as Amy Bloom's friend said), so that I can separate the wheat from the chaff. I need to get the clutter out of my life. Then I'll be able to see that which really matters and, thus, be able to give proper time to what really matters. But I can't do this until I've learned where my time is going, what I would like still to get out of life, and how to make a reasonable balance between the two.

It would be audacious of me to try to do this for you. In truth, it's hard enough to do it for myself. But let me analyze four areas of life where we can invest time and hope that the guidelines I suggest for these may help us in evaluating other possible areas of time-investment.

Let me begin with relationships. I start here because I am convinced that no other element of life is more important and no other use of time is more sacred. Use this time well, and you will be wiser in what you do with the rest of time.

The crucial relationship, beyond all others, is our relationship with God. You may want to discount what I'm saying because you've heard that I'm a preacher and a seminary teacher. In truth, it's the other way around. I'm a preacher because I was fortunate early in my life to begin a vital relationship with God. The longer I live the more certain I am that my relationship with God influences all my other relationships. My relationship with God will not guarantee the quality of my human relationships, but it will help make me a better, more patient, more loving participant in the human part.

So I'm trying these days to find more time to devote exclusively to God and to improve the quality of that time. I have always given early morning time to devotion, before going to work; now I've added to the time. This time includes both prayer and reading, and the reading includes both Bible and devotional writers. I won't tell you my devotional writers, because they change from year to year. Also I've learned that what blesses other people doesn't necessarily bless me, so there's no reason to think that what lifts my soul will also lift yours.

But the relationship with God is like every other relationship, it requires time and cultivation. The rule from Proverbs for human friendship also applies to the divine friendship; those who would have friends must show themselves friendly. And friendship takes time. That shouldn't surprise us. The higher the worth, the higher the price.

As for human relationships, I have become more intentional in taking care of them and more thoughtful in evaluating them. If someone's health or age indicates that the possibility of time with that person is likely to be limited, factor this into the friendship. So, too, if we know we're in an area for only a limited time. These two statements are only common sense, but somehow we forget that common sense also operates in those areas of life that are preciously uncommon.

I have talked about friendship in an earlier chapter; so I won't enlarge on it here except to underline its importance and to encourage us to keep seeking new friends because friends of the past keep slipping from us by one path or another. And especially treat all human relationships as sacred, all the way from a wave to a passing motorist, to our relationship with family members, or a friend we feel we'd die for. Human beings are made in God's image, and no matter how marred that image may be, the person may reveal something of God to us, or we to them. Thus every human relationship, even the most incidental, has a sacredness to it.

Second, take time to read (or to be read to if vision is limited). I'm sure I'm a fanatic about this, but let me exercise my fanaticism. I know of no operational gift to us humans that is lovelier than the gift of reading. I've sometimes said that if I'm alone and there's nothing else to read, I'll read the back of the cereal box. As it happens, however, I'm becoming more selective every day. I realize I'll never have time to read all the books I want to read, so I'm carefully eliminating the marginal—even while reminding myself that what seems dispensable today may become very attractive tomorrow.

Receive suggestions from friends, airport strangers, and book reviews, but be wise enough to dispense with most of them. You've developed some tastes of your own; no doubt you can improve on them, but have respect for who you are. Read for both pleasure and profit, and you'll often discover that the two are close kin. Turn off television, close down the internet, and read some classic from a century ago; it will be more relevant and more satisfying than either the television or the internet.

In earlier years you read what was assigned to you, by a teacher or professor or by the demands of your daily work. Start now to read some of the really fine things that you didn't have time for earlier. Read with pleasure. After all, you now know better what you really like and what for you is most worthwhile. I'm currently on a binge of some solid biographies, familiar essays, and semipopular literary criticism. But I won't tell you the authors because you might buy the book and discover that it's a waste of time for you. I've told you my current bent just to let you know how one's taste may unfold.

In a sense, if you love books you will never be lonely. But unfortunately, when you find something in a book that strikes a vital chord, you want desperately to discuss it with some other human being. I may be speaking only for myself, however. When I'm idling in a book store, I note that I run into both very friendly and very unfriendly people. Perhaps some readers prefer making friendships exclusively with books. And don't worry about knowing everything. Susanna Wesley, the wise mother of John and Charles and seventeen other children, advised John that "there are many truths it is not worthwhile to know." A quite different personality in our own day, the master of the familiar essay, Joseph Epstein, puts it this way, "I am pleased—proud even—never to have heard Howard Stern or Don Imus on the radio, but I'm a little sad to have to admit that I know who they are."[3] Some things only clutter the mind.

Third, there is travel. Spiritually I am a descendant of Abraham. "He went out without knowing where he was going" (Hebrews 11:8). I'm not quite that much of a traveler, but I'm altogether at home in airports and hotels. I've reached a point in life where I prefer comfortable hotels, but this doesn't mean overly expensive, because the cost distracts from my comfort.

Travel while you can. Many years ago I read a book about "The Inklings," that remarkable group of Christian writers, including C. S. Lewis, Tolkien, and Charles Williams, who met regularly to eat, drink, and talk. I learned of their holidays—the two or three day weekends the British cherish—and of how they would walk several hours until they reached a village pub for tea, then walking to another village for lunch,, and so on until an inn where they'd spend the night, talking all the way. I resolved that someday I would find a friend or two and follow such paths in rural England. But I allowed other things to claim my time, and I never made such a trip. Now the distance between the villages would seem prohibitive and I don't know who would put up with my lack of speed in walking. I'm sorry!

But see where you are, wherever it may be. That wonderful iconoclast, Henry David Thoreau, wrote, "I have traveled a good deal in Concord." Indeed, Thoreau saw more in the village of Concord than many tourists see in a tour of Europe. Travel like a child, allowing yourself to see wonders everywhere. Listen to the people wherever you go; they may not necessarily be knowledgeable, but you'll learn from them.

Fourth, spend time thinking. God has given you a mind. It may be a much better mind than you realize. It is altogether possible that it's a mind you've left largely undeveloped while concentrating on your career. One of my favorite people, to whom I've referred elsewhere, is Father Kilian McDonnell, a Benedictine monk. For forty-five years he wrote scholarly theological works, then one day at seventy-five while reading a poem in *The New Republic* said, "I think I can do as well," and set out to learn how, and then to do it.[4] In the years since then he has turned out several books of poetry that make one think, pray, and smile. But he had to think beyond his education and his stated vocation in order to do it.

The truth is, all of us think. That's what the mind does. I haven't read any studies on the matter, but I have a notion that the mind keeps thinking the way the heart keeps beating: It does so whether we tell it to or not. The difference is in those who direct the mind to think and in the direction they give it.

Some of our thinking is downright destructive. Of course I'm speaking of those who contemplate murder or violent revenge or who live in the world of sexual fantasy. But I have something else in mind. It is such a waste of the human brain to occupy it with resentment, bitterness, anger, or self-loathing. Not only are such thoughts unfit residents for the human mind, if they occupy the mind long enough they will slowly deteriorate the health of our bodies.

So be very wise and very selective in what you think about. There's no such thing as an idle thought; the thought may come at an idle time, but it quickly becomes active. Don't let the mind wander unduly in old hurts. It's hard to control the situation when someone subjects us to a monologue on the telephone, at the adjoining airplane seat, or at a social occasion, but it isn't hard to control when the monologue is in our own thought life. It's pretty foolish to subject oneself to an inner monologue that is repetitive, dull, time-wasting, and generally stupid.

We're all susceptible to nonproductive thinking. The apostle Paul urged his followers to "capture every thought to make it obedient to Christ" (2 Corinthians 10:5). A great preacher of a past generation spoke of "the expulsive power of a new affection." I have in my thought-file a collection of pleasant memories, of people and occasions and conversations. When my mind goes into negative gear, I turn to my file of pleasant thoughts and run them on the screen of my mind. It's my mind; why should I let garbage take control of it?

Who knows? If you start thinking more consciously you may come up with a poem, dream up a new cake recipe, or figure out a way to turn off the television without using the remote. Your mind is such a lovely place, and it's the one location that no one else can enter without your permission.

To grow older should mean, for sure, to realize the importance of redeeming the time. It doesn't mean to run faster or try to do more things; it means to use time to its highest and most fulfilling purposes. If you start living this way, you're getting very wise—whether you're eighty or fifty or seventeen—because you're redeeming God's unique gift. Time.

CHAPTER 9

I'm Not the Person
I Used to Be

Perhaps you've noticed that our chapters take their titles
from a wide variety of places, including the Bible, songs,
poems, and common sayings. This chapter is a phrase I've
heard scores or hundreds of times, but I can't trace its origin
in any of the standard books of quotations. Perhaps it's not

significant enough to have won such a place, though it seems to me to be as good as many I find there.

This phrase often comes in subdivisions of the subject, as when an athlete says, "I'm not the player I used to be," or a trumpeter confesses, "I don't have the lip I once had," or the vocalist declares, "My high notes aren't what they once were." But mostly we hear the phrase in a broader, more inclusive sense, the one that we speak as we feel that advancing years are taking command of our lives in a more insistent way; it may be primarily a particular skill, our hearing or vision, our endurance, or our general appearance and bearing. One way or another, one area of life or another—physical, mental, social—we feel that we're less in control or that we've reached a place where we're having to abandon some of our dreams.

Some say that this sense of change is the particular hazard of middle age. The man who once dreamed of playing ball in the big leagues slowly realizes that he's now being moved down in the batting order on the church softball team. And the woman who sometimes thought as she stood privately before a full length mirror that she had a chance at Miss America now notices that the clothes she has to wear make her look old, and the ones she'd like to wear make her look foolish.

But what happens when middle no longer seems the right adjective to describe one's age? What happens when in general one confesses to oneself, "I'm not the person I used to be"? What then?

Well, to begin with, congratulate yourself. You're playing in the big leagues now. This is no longer basketball with lower baskets, it's no longer a game where they don't keep score. This growing-up business isn't for wimps. Think of this testimony from an older person:

> I was young and now I'm old,
>   but I have never seen
>   the righteous left all alone,
> have never seen their children
>   begging for bread (Psalm 37:25).

You have to have lived a while to make such a statement, and you have to have a certain toughness in evaluating life if you're to do so. That testimony tells as much about the person who wrote it as it does about what he had observed. He knew he was no longer young because he now had a vantage point in life that was impossible when he was younger. His age was a declaration of fact, not a burden. He was able to see some things that most people could not see Not only because he had lived longer and had thus had more time for first-hand, in-depth research, but also because he was old enough to evaluate what he was observing.

That is, I'm not the person I used to be and I'm glad of it. Because if I were the person I used to be, I wouldn't understand what I'm seeing now. It's what I "used to be" that equips me for what I am now. It would be as foolish of me to regret that I'm no longer young as for a flower in full bloom to resent no longer being a bud.

Then, as you look at your present state, become your friend and not your adversary. I'm not telling you to fool yourself; it's true that you're no longer sixteen, but read the advantages in where you are rather than the disparagements. The language we hear and the language we speak shapes all of us. I reject, therefore, the phrase so many employ when they can't recall a name: "I'm having a senior moment." I remind myself, first, that we've had those moments since kindergarten, when in the midst of reporting the day to a parent we couldn't remember the name of a classmate. Do we have those moments more frequently as we grow older? No doubt. But I don't see it as a senior moment, I see it as data overload.

Here's what I mean. If a visitor comes into the seminary where I've spent the last nearly twenty years of my life and asks me the office location for a particular faculty member, I have to sort through the three offices he's had in the years I've known him. If I had come to the seminary only a year or two ago, I could give the inquirer a quick answer, because I would have known him for only one office. I sometimes attach a wrong last name to a given one. Why not? I've known scores of Allens, Alans, and Allyns in my lifetime; no wonder my God-given computer sometimes attaches a wrong surname. If someone smiles at your error you will be tempted to answer, "If you knew as much as I do, you too would have a hard time remembering it all." You won't say this of course, because you're old enough to know that it is not only an unkind answer, but it is also a self-defeating one.

Rejoice in the skills of time and experience. Baseball's best fastball pitchers know that when they lose some of their speed, they can rely more on their experience. The quarterback who is now half-a-second slower in his release of the football can read defenses in a way that makes up the difference. The woman who was once known for her clever put-downs now wins by her deeper understanding of human personality. Those who are growing older learn to claim the territory that is now theirs; those who have grown old see only what they once had.

Take advantage of your memory. Popular discussion and experience has made much of the issue of memory loss that comes with age. Part of this popular theory is true, in matters of names and dates and the reason for which we came into the kitchen or the family room. But Barry Gordon, a professor of neurology and cognitive science at the Johns Hopkins Medical Institutions, has another story to tell. He notes that our brains have an ability to store up ideas and then to connect those ideas to form new ideas.

Dr. Gordon calls this brain-skill "intelligent memory," probably because it shows itself so often in creative and imaginative ways. I know Dr. Gordon's term is better, but from a pragmatic point of view I have come to call this function "associative memory" because of the way it brings together pieces of information in the vast storehouse of the brain and relates them to one another. Even more exciting, this "intelligent memory" takes something out of a storage bin from fifty or seventy-five years ago and relates it to the news of the day, to events in one's private life, or in the circle of friendship.[1]

There is happy news. Dr. Gordon concludes that intelligent memory doesn't fade; rather, it can improve with age, because of the accumulated experiences of life. However, I must add that this benefit—like so many of life's benefits—has its perils. I observe it in many older people and each time I do I remind myself that I must not let this happen to me. I'm not usually in danger in ordinary conversation, because I am not an aggressive conversationalist. I can sit in a social gathering for an hour and say nothing unless somebody asks my opinion. But in a classroom or in a question and answer session during a lecture, I can go from one associative memory to another until my comments sound like a reading from *Finnegan's Wake*, especially when the concluding sentence ties up in some peculiar way with the place where I began. Perhaps this is why older people sometimes seem garrulous, their connective, intelligent memory is dangerously unlimited. Nevertheless, it's a wonderful gift, and I am unceasingly grateful for Dr. Gordon's studies.

This brings us to a moral factor of growing older. In the massive collection of human experience that goes into any person's years of living, there is a substantial element of mistakes which make a surprisingly good foundation for building a better future. The late Peter Gomes, for so many years the Dean of Chapel at Harvard University, said that "the remembrance of disorder is therapeutic." He continued, "The logic here is that if we remember, or are reminded, of where we have gone wrong, we will learn from our mistakes not to repeat them, and from false starts or errors we will make progress in the right direction."[2] Most of us are inclined to use our errors as a basis for advising other people. And incidentally this practice is not limited to older people. We love to have people profit from our experience. It's a generous impulse, but it's not often particularly effective. Unless someone asks for our help, we do well to concentrate on how we can turn yesterday's sins, blunders, and errors into making something better from our own lives. Perhaps then people will ask our guidance.

I find great encouragement in a word from the nineteenth century pulpit giant, Phillips Brooks. "You must learn, you must let God teach you, that the only way to get rid of your past is to make a future out of it. God will waste nothing." Some of our past is thrust upon us by others. In the worst scenario, others may intend to hurt us. Still more of our past, in most cases, is of our own doing, some of it the product of our sins, some of our immaturity, some simply of good ideas and good plans gone wrong. In the end, however, the issue is not from whence the bad stuff in our past came, but how we deal with it. It is quite astonishing what a solid foundation can be built from the accumulated waste of the past. And this, as Dr. Brooks said, is because "God will waste nothing." We do well if we join God in the reclamation project called

"The Future" in which some of the best material is found in the failures and, yes, even the sins, of the past.

I have a friend who knows he's not the man he used to be, and he counts it off daily. "Today is 12,263," he wrote me several months ago. He is counting back to the time when, as he puts it, "I was a dead man suffering from the terminal disease of alcoholism. But God's munificent grace and gratuitous power came down and literally saved my life. I have been sober one day at a time now for over 33 years. Every single day is a gift."

I applaud my friend Bill, because he is building on his past, one day at a time. He has learned that every day is a gift. If you learn that, so that you enter every morning thanking God for a new day, you're a rich person. Some people, because of despair and hopelessness, don't know that every day is a gift, and others are dull to that fact because of their arrogance. They're poor, so very poor. Bill knows God's grace and power. If you learn that, whether you learn it from alcoholism, as Bill has, or from repeated failures with your temper, your ego, or your thought life, you are a better person than you were, and richer by divine measure. And you can say with joy and gratitude, "I'm not the person I used to be."

More than twenty years go I had dinner one evening in the home of a retired Buick dealer in a small town in upstate New York. He had opened his dealership soon after World War II. He said with a smile, "When old-timers say to me, 'A car isn't what it used to be,' I always answer, 'And aren't you glad!' " I knew what he was talking about, because I can remembered the days when one took a car in for oil change and lubrication every thousand miles. And each time one bought gasoline at what we then called a service station (now *there* was a loss), the attendant checked the water, the oil, and the tires because it was likely that one or the other needed attention. My host was right: I'm glad my automobile isn't what it used to be.

And this is the way I feel about us human beings. The goal is not to remain young. The goal is to grow up. And the measure of growing up is that we've become better persons. As persons we inhabit physical bodies, therefore we should treat those bodies with respect and, indeed, with awe because they're a gift from God. Christians should not be content, therefore, to allow their bodies to grow slovenly and undisciplined. But even under the best of care our bodies will come in time to suffer some limitations: we won't run as fast, if at all, we won't jump as high, if at all, and the skin won't be quite as smooth or unblemished.

But the inner person! This is quite another matter. So the apostle Paul, whose body had suffered beatings, tough living, imprisonments and being stoned, would write, "But even if our bodies are breaking down on the outside, the person that we are on the inside is being renewed every day. Our temporary minor problems are producing an eternal stockpile of glory for us that is beyond all comparison" (2 Corinthians

4:16-17). Paul therefore recommended that we stop focusing our attention on the things "that can be seen" because those things "don't last, but the things that can't be seen are eternal" (4:18).

And here indeed is where we should hope and pray that we're not the person we used to be. It's natural that we humans think so much about that which passes away, because those things are so visible; and in our contemporary culture they are also so trumpeted and glorified. But if we're growing up, truly growing up, we realize increasingly that there is much more to us than this. Jesus' parable of the rich man and Lazarus makes that point: During his lifetime Lazarus had almost nothing of the visible and the rich man had it all, but at the end Lazarus was rich and the rich man was eternally, devastatingly poor (Luke 16:19-31). the tale of the Pharisee and the publican at prayer echoes this theme. The Pharisee thought he had it made and he had evidence to prove it. While the publican realized that his soul was destitute, and he too had evidence to make his point. But in all that mattered, the Pharisee was in poverty and the publican was on the edge of eternal riches (Luke 18:9-14).

If we have simply grown *old*, we lose the joy of our human potential. If we see ourselves as a finished product, a person who is already as kind, as intelligent, as gentle and forgiving, and as generous as we'll ever get to be—well, then, in truth we're in sad shape. But if we see ourselves as wiser than we were, kinder, more in control of ourselves (even if by minimal measures) and see that we're *still growing* (that is, that we're growing *older*, not *old*)—ah, then! Not only are we not the person we used to be, we're not the person we're going to be.

And that's a lovely prospect! I'd hate to stop where I am now. I belong to a faith tradition—Methodism—that historically made much of the fact that one needed to be perfect when one entered heaven. This perfection is the work of the Holy Spirit, but we're expected to cooperate. So, in Methodist language, I'm "going on to perfection."

So when you're looking at some of the areas of your life, especially those that are easily visible or more accessible to conventional measure—the state of your body, perhaps, or when you're reminiscing on the glory days of leadership in church, community or career—and you start to lament, "I'm not the person I once was," look at the data more carefully. Add, "And I'm glad, because I'm a more complete person now than I was then."

Then, two more short sentences. "And I don't intend to stop here. Because God isn't done with me yet."

CHAPTER 10

WHEN THE SHADOWS
ARE DARK AND DEEP

If this is to be an honest book I must include a chapter on a subject I know about mostly at second hand. What about growing older when most of the days and nights are spent in a place of dark, deep shadows? I'm speaking of the kind of life marked by almost constant physical suffering or perhaps the kind of degenerative disease which takes a person's physical or mental powers piece by piece, day by day, while our best medical science confesses that they have no answer? I think, too, of those persons who struggle with their personal demons of agonizing depression, despair, or self-loathing. In earlier years they coped with this darkness by work and the excitements of family and social life, but now there seems little or no escape. Can one still grow older under such circumstances, or should one concede that one is simply painfully old with no other exit than death?

I repeat, I know most of this subject at secondhand. In a sense, it has been a broad and sensitive secondhand, because I spent most of my adult life as a parish pastor, an intentionally faithful one. Even while serving as senior minister in churches of rather large membership, I visited regularly not only in hospitals but also in nursing homes and the world of the permanently shut-in. But I know well enough that listening to the stories of pain and living with pain are quite different matters; and that while a good pastor or dear friend can enter into another person's pain so that at times it seems like one's own, one can also step out of it. For those afflicted, it is a permanent residence.

I've been blessed with quite good health. I've had some surgery along the way, including a type of surgery that could well have taken from me the work I loved. Thanks to a skilled surgeon and God's mercy, I came through perfectly. Mostly, however, my physical health has been excellent. I marvel that this is so when I consider the unbalanced diet on which I grew up during the Great Depression. As for mental and social health, I have wrestled with my demons, but I have survived and, indeed, have grown. So I write this chapter cautiously, knowing that I don't know what you've gone through, what you are going through just now, or what you're on the verge of going into. And I know something else: That even if you and I had passed through the same illness it wouldn't be quite the same because you and I are different. Thus the illness or emotional pressures that might break my spirit would only invigorate yours. The darkness of the valley depends partially on the vision of the traveler. The stone that stumbles one may for another be nothing more than a means of climbing a little higher.

But having said that I must go on to say that all we can know about life's dark and deep valleys is by the experiences of those who have already gone through them or who are currently doing so. In some details they may respond differently than you or I would, but the variance is still within the same territory of experience, so we can learn from our fellow travelers.

Perhaps the most astonishing thing I've learned, whether as pastor and counselor or by way of my reading, is the remarkable degree of victory. There are few thoroughly sad songs among those who have spent late years in the valley of shadows. The unsurprising thing is that a large percentage of those who are coping well are persons with a deep religious faith. This observation is not a product of what you may see as my prejudiced point of view, but the conclusion of a substantial number of surveys by persons who are seen as objective scholars. The disappointing thing is that not all those who profess to be religious are victorious in their outlook. This may reflect the level of their religious faith, or it may indicate further that we humans are all made differently, For some personality-types the struggle is simply much more complex than for others.

So I think of a truly grand husband and wife, both medical doctors, who spent their entire careers as missionary doctors in the Far East. I came to know them after their return to the States. Their health deteriorated rather quickly, including their vision. All of life was a struggle. The wife observed in nearly every letter of her later years that she had no sympathy with Browning's lines about "the best is yet to be." For her, each day was a battle both physically and emotionally; she hated being old. More recently, I think of a man who enjoyed substantial success in his business and with it a wide-ranging social life. Now he is in the first stages of Alzheimer's, and the time ahead is foreboding. No wonder he said the other day, "If I could find the man that said these are the golden years, I'd like to hang him." I've not been in the shoes of either of these persons. I'm not about to pass judgment on them. But I know there are other witnesses from the same world of dark and deepening shadows.

One of the greatest souls I've ever known I first met when

he was in his late eighties. I came upon him in our seminary library. I was looking for a book I needed for my work. He was simply trying to pursue some research for the continuing growth of his own soul. We became friends that day, and each time we visited I became a better man. Soon after his ninety-first birthday he wrote to thank me for something or other. "My mobility is failing," he observed, "but in the ways that really matter, I am, I hope, improving." If he had wanted to, he could also have observed that his vision was failing, as evidenced by the large scrawl in hi penmanship, but he saw no need to list his ailments or restrictions.

He also was revealing one of the major secrets of living well in the midst of a dark and more constricted place: He was making adjustments. Rather than railing against his decreasing mobility, he was concentrating on what he was sure mattered most, his character and his mind. Joseph Sittler concluded that there is a time when what we need is "courage, acquiescence, resignation, acceptance . . . a movement of the total spirit from an anxious hanging-on to a graceful letting-go; a releasement."[1] Sittler, a consummate scholar and lover of books and learning, wrote this when his sight was essentially gone. He was writing from an adjustment that he had made and would continue to make for as long as he lived. Because adjustments are not simply decisions, they are a way of life to which we commit ourselves.

Adjustment! I find it too in another friend, writing to me when she was 89 and in what she described as "very fragile health." I could hardly imagine her being fragile in anything. She was for many years on the editorial staff of a daily newspaper in a university community, and a world traveler who regaled community clubs throughout the state in lectures reporting on her travels. Now she was restricted to her apartment, reduced to "black and white" by contrast with the "old days." But she continued, "You would be proud of me. I concentrate on the good things. I am very mentally alert and have excellent eyesight and hearing. I thank God day and night." She had adjusted to the loss of some things that had once been the mountain peaks of her life, but she was concentrating on what she had left.

As I have said before, our culture urges us to prepare financially for our later years. The Social Security program compels a certain degree of preparation, and various tax laws make it profitable for us to lay aside money for retirement. But no law can compel us to prepare our souls and minds for the future. Come to think of it, I haven't heard many sermons on the subject.

It's strange, isn't it, that we give so much thought to whether in our later years we'll have enough money to survive, yet seldom ask ourselves if we'll have enough spirit to keep us going. A variety of private and government insurance programs will keep us alive and tended to physically as we grow older, but what will take care of our souls, so we'll be able to ride life's rough waves with a measure of poise?

And those admirable financial advisors: They tell us to

estimate how much we'll need to live on after we reach a certain age, and they tell us—correctly—that we won't need as much money for some elements of living as we need in our early and middle years. They advise us to consider how we can, and should, cut back financially as we grow older. Is it not equally wise to consider in advance how we might cut back with age in other factors of life? How will we manage if our physical, social, cultural or intellectual lives are made smaller?

It's good to invest in wisdom and humor, because they pay high dividends as we grow older. R. R. Reno asked an older friend with health problems how he was doing. The friend shrugged, sighed, and answered, "Sometimes wisdom comes with age, but more often than not it's just age that comes with age."[2] I smiled as I read it and said to myself that the man had also gotten wisdom even as he discredited it; that's what provided him with his clever response.

Oscar Wilde was still a relatively young man when he died at 46, penniless, in a hotel in Paris. He wrote to a friend, "I am dying as I have lived — beyond my means." Someone paraphrased Wilde: "You taught me that wisdom can come only with winter."[3]

Some Catholic biographers note Wilde's returning in his last days to the faith of his upbringing. The winter of life came early for him, but there is evidence that while losing public esteem and the previous security of his literary career he did indeed gain some wisdom and kept his razor-like humor.

But beyond humor and wisdom, there is faith. Indeed, humor and wisdom find their roots in faith. Samuel Wesley, father of John and Charles, the founders of the Methodism movement, was himself a man of deep faith. He lived most of his adult life and ministry in an inland village, Epworth, in Lincolnshire, England. He suffered a great deal of pain in his last days, in a world where pain relievers were hardly known. But when his son John asked about his pain during Samuel's dying hours the old man answered, "God does chasten me with pain; yea, all my bones with strong pain; but I thank Him for all, I bless Him for all, I love Him for all." I don't think I would see pain as God's chastening, but I am in awe of Samuel Wesley's readiness to thank God even for his pain and to love God for it.

I have seen such faith up close. I remember an early winter day on a farm in Wisconsin more than half a century ago. I had called on the young mother, in her mid-thirties, her youngest child barely a year old, now great not with another child but with a cancer. We walked together into the late afternoon cold, she on her way to an errand in the barn and I on my way to my car. I didn't feel that my pastoral conversation had helped as much as I had wanted it to, nor my prayer. I inquired again about her feelings. She smiled, pointed to her extended stomach — "this thing," she called it, "this thing growing inside me." She was still holding on, in no way diminished in courage or faith. The "thing" won before the winter was over, but not really. She died with grace and strength, a grand bequest to her husband, her widowed mother, and her small children.

Cancer: It's a four-letter word spelled with six letters, and our culture finds it harder to speak than any of the declared four-letter words. I think of a preacher friend in Pennsylvania, a man honored by his colleagues and parishioners, who fought cancer for three and a half years before it took his life. To the end, when people asked how he was feeling, he would answer, "I'm doing great except for this bit of cancer." He didn't allow cancer to name him.

One of the most foreboding and mysterious illnesses of our time is Alzheimer's. We've had a name for it for just over a century, but as one of the premier specialists in the field has said, there are still more questions than answers. One thing is sure, Alzheimer's is no respecter of persons. Not long ago one of America's most respected theologians sent a note to a fellow scholar. "I want to inform you that I am now middle stage Alzheimer's. I will not be able to do my writing, etc. I am 73 years now. I've enjoyed my biblical three score and ten. I am not bitter. I have had a good life. I'll meet you over Jordan if not before. You are free to make this news known."[4] He wanted to declare his faith while he was still able to speak for himself, if I may put it that way, before the disease garbled his speech. He wrote with the calm certainty of those who know whom they have believed and who know that God is capable of keeping them, even when they no longer know they are being kept.

And then there is ALS (Amyotrophic Lateral Sclerosis), "Lou Gehrig's Disease," as it is commonly known. Few diseases are more cruel. It is as if the human body had decided to execute itself in the most deliberate and devastating way possible. My friend Jim was both a fine musician and an outstanding pastor. He served churches with excellence and true godliness until his retirement, and in his retirement he and his wife poured their Christian love into the neediest places they could find until Jim discovered he had ALS.

In our several afternoon visits over iced tea his illness was only a matter for preliminary reporting, along with recent travels and the other minutiae of life, after which we could plunge into the fun of lively conversation. The time came when Jim and his wife accepted the invitation of their sons to move to another city where they could be near family. There, a few weeks before Jim's death, his wife wrote to old friends that his lung capacity had shrunk from 87 percent in the spring to 46 percent in the fall, and then had gone down rapidly to 26 percent, at which point they began hospice.

"We are managing well," Jim's wife wrote, "and God's grace has proven to be totally sufficient even for this leg of the journey. (We have preached God's grace all these years, so it shouldn't be a surprise that it's the 'real deal' now.)"

Yes, for sure, "the real deal." This faith in Christ is good not only for summer days in the sunshine, but also for the storms that come to most of our lives.

I have given more time in this chapter to stories of persons who have lived victoriously in latter years when the shadows have been dark and deep, and especially people whom I have known personally. I could have drawn on almost endless reports from the Bible and from history and biographies, but I chose purposely to select a few at close hand. Believe me, I had plenty to choose from. I have seen a great deal of nobility in action, much of it known only to the few who were in the family or a circle of friendship.

I believe we can best prepare for the place of shadows if we prepare ourselves in the days of sunshine and mild storms. Again our spiritual security is not unlike financial security: Save up in the days of enough so that you will have reserves to draw upon in days of loss. But don't save spiritually for just that reason. Enjoy the goodness of God, the wonders of grace, and the astonishing faithfulness of our Lord every day. Know that if you do, you will be ready in some measure for every tomorrow. Dietrich Bonhoeffer, the towering martyr of World War II, is worthy of quoting at this point because he knew whereof he spoke. "I believe," Bonhoeffer wrote, "that God will give us all the strength we need to help us to resist in all time of distress. But he never gives it in advance, lest we should rely on ourselves and not on him alone."[5]

Live well now, and trust tomorrow with the God with whom you walk today. That God will still be with you tomorrow.

CHAPTER 11

THERE'S MORE TO LIFE THAN TWO FRONT TEETH

Let me go back to the scene in our opening chapter, the memory of my luncheon host in that small town in northwest Iowa. He was telling me that the Bible was right in saying that life after three score years and ten is "labor and sorrow"; in his eighties, he felt that he knew by experience. Somehow his limited dental equipment—two front teeth, one upper, one lower—symbolized his story for me. He was managing somehow, but it wasn't the way as a nineteen-year-old that I wanted to live out my days.

Nevertheless, something began to dawn on me that day, though I'm sure it was some time before the idea took root fully. I now realize that my philosophical host was a living contradiction to his own declarations. True, his body wasn't what it once was, but his inviting me to have lunch with him was evidence that he was alive, somewhat well, and wonderfully hospitable. He also thoughtfully realized that the visiting preacher might not be faring well for his noon meals. There was an ice cream parlor in that small town, but I don't remember a restaurant. He was still adventuresome, too. He apparently thought it might be fun to talk with someone one-fourth his age. I was quite willing to let him speak, but he insisted on pursuing my thoughts, giving me the unwarranted impression that my ideas mattered. And he was still evaluating life and arguing with what he saw. He confessed that the psalmist was right, but he didn't like it.

In truth, except for his tooth shortage he was in many respects better equipped to enjoy life than when he was forty or fifty—to say nothing of when he was fifteen. You see, much of our best enjoyment of life is by way of comparison. We say as we finish a particularly good meal, "This is one of the best meals I've ever had." How would we know a good meal, to say nothing of a better one, if we'd never eaten before? Our pleasure is enhanced by our ability to compare, and the more one has lived the better the quality and fulfillment in the comparing. That is, the ability to distinguish, to evaluate quality, is an essential factor in the best enjoying and apprehending of life.

I suspect that herein lies some of the frustration parents and grandparents feel in the privileges they give to their children. We take the child sight-seeing or to some event, and expect them to feel the thrill we do—or the thrill we think we recall from our earlier experience. Sometimes the child or teenager's response is less than cataclysmic. How could it be otherwise? They have little or no basis of comparison. And of course if we try to remember how we felt when we had the same experience, we forget that our coloring of the occasion is now wonderfully augmented by memory and sentiment.

That is, we have more capacity to enjoy life as we grow older. Mind you, I'm not ignoring our losses. Some of us don't see as well or hear as well as we used to, and some lose the acuity in their taste buds so that food doesn't excite or satisfy as it once did—to say nothing of the fact that in later years we don't often have the chance to work up a good appetite. But what we've lost is made up for by what we've gained, and if we would concentrate less on what we've lost and more on the gain, we'd come out very well.

We gain the ability to distinguish not simply between the

good and the bad, but also between the good and the better, and the better and the best. If we're reasonably wise we become more cautious about the superlatives we use because we've seen or experienced enough to know that we may have forgotten some comparable experience. Also we now know that there are persons who've experienced things that we haven't. I realize now that my parents' generation was onto something when they concluded discussions by saying, "When you get as old as I am, you'll know better." Very true, simply because with time, one has a greater background of comparative experience. It's very hard to judge anything unless one has a plumb line of comparison by which to measure it. The greatest music? What varieties have you heard? The greatest public speaker? Did you hear Franklin Delano Roosevelt say, "We have nothing to fear"? The greatest baseball player? Did you ever see Willie Mays, Joe DiMaggio, or Ted Williams? (Just to name a few comparators.) As we grow older we shouldn't get stuck in the rut of "there's nothing to compare with the past," but we should rejoice that we've lived long enough and experienced enough to have a basis of comparison and with it an increased ability to distinguish between the average, the good, and the exceptional.

With this, those who are growing older have a greater capacity to do good. Cicero (106–43 B.C.), that remarkable Roman wise man, contended, "Great deeds are not done by strength or speed or physique. They are the products of thought, and character, and judgment. And far from diminishing, such qualities actually increase with age."[1] We gain common sense about what things matter most. We may well have less energy, perhaps in some ways less ability, to accomplish many things. But the odds are good that we have far better insight about what matters most, and we see more clearly how to achieve our goals. We have, in the language of Cicero, more thought, character, and judgment.

One of the best ways to employ our thought, character, and judgment is in listening to other people. Loneliness is a particular bane of old age. As one's contemporaries exit by death or by moving to a location nearer their families, the circle of conversation grows smaller. Fewer people recognize the names of athletes, entertainers, political leaders, authors, or comic strips that once filled our lives, so life gets lonely. What then?

The answer is simple. Become a good listener. The world is dying for attentive listeners, people who tune in their ears and their souls when the other person speaks. I sometimes think that the world of paid listeners—psychologists, psychiatrists, and counselors—came into their own when the third generation moved out of our homes: the generation of grandparents, maiden aunts, and bachelor uncles. We humans need skilled listeners. We need persons who listen with empathy, who know how to ask evocative questions, and who are warmly curious about us.

And with that knowledge we can enter into one of life's most important and least practiced occupations: prayer. As we know more about other people, about the things that burden them, frustrate them, bring them joy, their dreams and anxieties and longings, we can become expert in prayer. One of the loveliest moments in the British television saga, *Downton Abbey*, comes when a war-bereaved father seeks the friendship of a daughter-in-law he has hardly had opportunity to know. But she is all he has left now that his only son has been killed in the Great War. When the young war widow wonders what value she can hold for this almost-unknown father-in-law he answers, "Without you, I'd have no one to pray for."

It is a great privilege—a divine and eternal privilege—to pray for others. If we believe with the English poet of another day, Alfred Lord Tennyson, "More things are wrought by prayer / Than this world dreams of," then what better way to invest our time than to pray? (Tennyson, "The Idylls of the King"). If your prayer list is short, extend it by listening. And if still it is short, follow the advice of one great soul who seeks to "pray for children whose pictures aren't on anyone's refrigerator door." I keep a place in my heart for the anonymous souls that life seems to have passed by. But start with the people you listen to. If you listen to people long enough, they'll conclude that you're very wise. And bless you, they'll be right!

And we should never forget a unique blessing in growing older, one that can be gotten no other way but which—unfortunately—we tend to avoid. That is, the awareness of death. As that delightful essayist, Joseph Epstein, puts it,

"We are all born with a serious and unalterable defect: We grow old—at least the lucky among us do—and then we die."[2] Since death is so assured, it will do us much good if we'll ponder it properly. The late Peter Gomes, for so many years Dean of the Chapel at Harvard University, said that "the awareness of death is the first key to the discipline that contributes to the good life."[3] Life is like football, it is a game played alongside a clock. Look, then, to the quarterback. I think it can be said that no ability is more important to a good quarterback than knowledge of the clock and how to manage time in light of that knowledge. A strong arm, scrambling feet, and a good eye for reading the defense are all wasted if the quarterback thinks he has three minutes left when in truth he has thirty seconds. All of us should develop a little of this instinct about the years of our lives. I repeat what I must have said before: There's nothing morbid about this. It's just good sense. Learn to manage the clock.

Some people learn this art early in life. They impress their peers—and in some cases, drive them to despair—by their ability to manage their time. It's interesting that in Samuel Johnson's prayers he so often repented of his misuse of time yet he noted that one thing he disliked about his contemporary, John Wesley, the founder of Methodism, was that Wesley never had time simply to talk; he was always on his way to do something. Thus Wesley left his clergy with the rule, "Never trifle away time; never spend any more time at any one place than is strictly necessary."

At this moment some older person wants to tell me that one of the blessings of retirement is that they no longer need to watch the clock. I understand the point. But this is actually part of the point I'm making. During the years when we are working at farm, office, profession or managing a household, other people control much of what we do with our time. Now, older, the time decisions are in one's own hands. There's a danger that we won't actually make any time-decisions; we'll simply follow the stream of the day, never really know where our time has gone. I'm urging that we look over a day's or a week's activity from time to time and ask the highly pertinent question, "Is this the best way to spend my remaining years? If not, what can I do about it?" I'm not recommending slavish attention to the clock, but a happy recognition that we are now, to a greater degree than at any time in our lives, the boss of our own time. With that the case, what is it that we really—after prayerful thought—want to do with our time? Because we've lived for a fair piece, we're now equipped to use time intelligently. Happily, we now have more time to use!

And with age we can come to the happy balance between resignation and insistence. This calls for a healthy tough-mindedness. There are some things one can't do any more or can't do well enough to merit the time they demand. Learn to be resigned to such. On the whole I fall asleep easily. But sometimes I keep myself awake fretting over things I can't change. I lie in bed composing letters to the editor that fortunately I will never write. I rail in my mind against injustices that are beyond my curing. Can I do something to change matters, in my own life or in my larger world? If so, begin working to that end. But if not, accept with resignation.

But at the same time, keep a healthy protest in the soul. Hold out for some dreams as long as possible, and give those dreams a chance for fulfillment. I speak a vigorous "Amen!" each time I read Kilian McDonnell's poem "Impatience at the Loom." Pondering Isaiah 38:12, "You cut me from the loom" McDonnell complains to God, "unfinished / at five and eighty."[4]

At age eighty-five, McDonnell is still insistent: "China is not yet visited." He wants still to go to China! Is it a ridiculous goal? Not necessarily. At the least it's a matter to bring into God's Complaint Department, and at best, perhaps it is a dream that can still come to pass. One of the beauties of growing older is that one is far better equipped to find the balance between resignation and insistence. The proper balance is spiritually and emotionally healthy. As we grow older, we can strike that balance. We learn what to give up and what experiences still to seek.

And with the passage of years there is the possibility that we will come to know who we are and to be satisfied with what we discover. In her book, "Why We Lie," Dorothy Rowe rejoices at age eighty, "I have reached an age where I no longer need to pretend I know everything."[5] It is definitely a great gain to be rid of such a burden, and it isn't likely to happen except as we come to a place of self-acceptance where we no longer feel driven to impress other people. Age alone doesn't bring this to pass, of course; so it is that some people simply become more assertive and demanding with age, as if they intend to make sure before they die that other people have come to appreciate them to the full measure of their worth.

Perhaps there are two kinds of people in the world: those who never receive the degree of appreciation they deserve and those whose hunger for appreciation is never satisfied no matter how much attention is paid to them. Both persons deserve sympathy but for very different reasons. Blessed is the person who, looking back on life, is able to make peace with what has been accomplished, with tasks undone that now cannot be done, and with whatever evaluation others may place on their lives.

With age we should come to know that the only real arbiter of our lives is God; no one else knows enough about whom we are and the influences with which we've lived to be qualified to pass judgment on us. Furthermore, neither do we. Even with all our self-searching we will never fully understand the stuff that makes up our person and that has influenced our lives and our decisions. This is the point at which we must make peace with God, the One who has gifted us and who knows most surely the stuff of which we're made. In making that peace with God we may realize that we need to clear away from the soul some garbage in past relationships; that is, we may need to make right with some persons we have hurt.

When that is done, rejoice in who you are. There's no need to impress anyone else. Most of the reason we try to impress others is because we're unsure of our own worth and we feel insecure unless certain other persons—perhaps many persons—praise us or make us feel important or needed. But with age we can know no one comes to the end with a perfect score and ultimately only God knows the score. That is, only God knows fully our gifts and our limitations; thus how well we've done with the unique stuff that makes up our person. The secret at this point in life is to right any wrongs that are remediable, repent of failures and sins while allowing God to grant forgiveness, and to recognize that if God accepts our efforts to clear the records no one else's opinion really matters. Who cares if the novice in the stands boos your effort if the Final Scorekeeper is pleased with your game?

My long-ago host was down to two teeth, but he was wealthier than he knew. Beginning with the fortitude that helped him get along with only two teeth, he was still managing each day with remarkable vigor and wisdom. There's no denying that we humans experience a variety of diminishing as we grow older. But if we are wise—wise with the wisdom that comes with years of living—we will discover that essentially every loss is a trade-off. And by God's grace, and with our cooperation, the ultimate score of growing older is a trade-gain.

It might also be said that a great many contemporary children are suffering from experience-overload. Their parents want so much for their children to have everything that they dull their undeveloped taste before the children have reached an age of enjoyment discernment.

CHAPTER 12

THE BEST IS
YET TO COME

A friend of mine—a retired minister, as it happens—lives on a welcoming mountain top in western North Carolina. The mountain isn't an Everest or even a Pike's Peak, but as we circled our way to the top I wondered when the road would end. When we pulled into his driveway on that August afternoon, I also wondered how long even the lightest snowfall or ice storm might isolate him. He disposed of my question with laughter. At this point in life, he doesn't mind being isolated for a few days now and then. Besides, he's named his home "Mount Nebo."

If you've forgotten about Mount Nebo (most people have), it is part of the story of that magnificent Old Testament hero, Moses. Moses has his place not only in the Scriptures but in a wide variety of human lore, as the first great emancipator, as the iconic lawgiver, and as a leader who could steer a fledgling nation through the wilderness for forty years. He was a man of remarkable humility and restraint, but one day he lost control of his own person and stepped unredeemably out of bounds. Next to pleasing God, Moses' greatest desire was to lead his people, the new nation of Israel, into the land of their promise, into Canaan. But because of one reckless decision, that door was closed to him. He pleaded with God and got one concession. He would not be able to enter Canaan, but God would accompany him to Mount Nebo, "the peak of the Pisgah slope," and there "the LORD showed him the whole land" (Deuteronomy 34:1).

As I see it, Mount Nebo is that wonderful place where, by the grace of God, we can look with new perception at what we have done, what we've failed to do, and what we wish we hadn't done, then look to God's promised land with peace and thanksgiving. When the writer of Deuteronomy tells us that when Moses died, "His eyesight wasn't impaired"

(34:7), I am quite sure he is speaking of Moses' physical ability to see; in our language, Moses died with twenty-twenty vision. But my soul reads more into the phrase. I believe Moses had the spiritual vision to look at the past with charity, the present with peace, and the future with eternal hope. He was free of the kind of spiritual astigmatism that sometimes blurs and confuses the images of the soul.

The view from Mount Nebo is magnificent. All this and heaven, too!

I don't think any of us compare ourselves with Moses in areas of achievement, but most of us understand something of his period of wilderness wandering. For some, forty years might sound like an accurate estimate. Most of us haven't been that bad off, but we may remember wandering years in a wilderness of changing college majors once or several times, and after that some career changes—perhaps several. Some students of the American scene predict that very few in the current generation will complete their working life in the career with which they began. It's not that they've gotten lost in the wilderness, but that our culture is now changing the boundaries of career, forcing us to re-work our plans once and again, and perhaps still again. For many there is the wilderness of a broken marriage or a dissembled friendship. For others the indefinable feeling that is captured only by the German *angst*, a word that gives us the feeling that we have a syllable to encompass what we can't really define. So yes, we know about wandering in the wilderness.

And we know, too, about decisions, choices, and mistakes that we can never fully mend. We can build something new from most of them, God helping us, but some of life's changes can find focus only by the gift of faith. Sometimes a tough kind of faith tells us that we will have to wait for our Canaan land before we will make full sense of the earthly story. To put the matter more clearly, to be sure you know where I'm headed, some answers will have to wait until heaven. As an unsophisticated hymn of my childhood promised, "we'll understand it better by and by . . . When all the saints of God are gathered home." It was a reassuring word for those days of the Great Depression. And if you're wondering: Yes, I believe in heaven. Obviously you don't have to agree with me, but I do so believe.

Meanwhile, if we choose at times to climb up Mount Nebo as we grow older (not *old*, just *older*), we will see some things we couldn't see before. We were in no position for discerning vision when we were still wandering in the wilderness of middle age or even in the transition years into Social Security. But it is the battles of the wilderness years that equip us so we can apprehend Mount Nebo when we get there. As I have mentioned earlier, Samuel Johnson celebrated new beginnings on his birthday, New Year's Day, and Easter; he loved to "start again." On New Year's Day when he was sixty years old, Johnson prayed, "Let my remaining days be innocent and useful."

I'm fascinated by the two adjectives Johnson used to

describe what he hoped his "remaining days" would be. I remind you that Johnson gave the English language its first truly complete dictionary, and that his dictionary was replete with instances of the way each particular word had been used by someone of literary or historical significance. With his innate love of learning, Johnson might well have asked that his latter days be marked by sophistication and by broader and more aggressive learning. Not so. As a man of piety, which he surely was, Johnson might have prayed for love and faith. But he didn't ask for these.

Instead, he asked for innocence and usefulness. Asking for innocence is asking to become childlike, unspoiled by the world, an interesting request indeed for a scholar, journalist, and what we today would call a newspaper columnist. And to be *useful?* Johnson knew better than most of us what that word could imply. He lived in a culture where a substantial number of people were employed as servants. He had servants of his own (whom he treated, incidentally, with gracious regard). If there was any definition for a servant, it was that he or she was *useful.* I submit that Samuel Johnson was well up Mount Nebo when he prayed that his remaining time might be "innocent and useful."

Two months before Samuel Moor Shoemaker's death he knew he was in his countdown. Profound gratitude marked his mood. For some twenty-seven years he was rector of Calvary Episcopal Church in New York City, a pulpit of far-reaching significance. He played a key role in helping the founders of Alcoholics Anonymous. His decade as rector of Calvary Episcopal Church in Pittsburgh became known nationally as The Pittsburgh Experiment, which became a model for hundreds of other churches across the nation. Looking back, he wrote, "It has been a great run. I wouldn't have missed it for the world." Not only was "the over-all experience of being alive . . . a thrilling experience," he was confident that "death is a doorway to more of it; clearer, cleaner, better, with more of the secret opened than locked."[1]

John Wesley and the first generation of Methodists liked to say that "the Methodists died well"; that is, that their faith was of such substance that crossing into the next world was itself a victory. In a time when most people died at home, medical science could do little to lengthen life, and sedation was uncommon, friends and family and fellow believers were often present at the hour of death. Mount Nebo was likely to be a community event, so to speak. Those who gathered to watch fellow believers die expected to see a good exit and perhaps a truly glorious one. John Wesley's last words were as simple and straight-forward as much of what he said: "The best of all is, God is with us."

But sometimes even the loveliest of souls can approach that mountain with uneasiness. Over a period of some fifteen years Professor David Snowdon carried on an in-depth study of 678 Catholic sisters, ranging in age from seventy-five to one hundred six, to learn more about Alzheimer's Disease. In the course of the study he came to know Sister Laura, who earlier was misdiagnosed as having Alzheimer's and lived under that burden for four years before a perceptive nurse saw to tests that demonstrated that she was by no means so afflicted. Later Sister Laura confided to Professor Snowdon, "Dr. Snowdon, do you know what my worst fear was?" At this point her eyes filled with tears. "That I was going to forget Jesus," she said. "I finally realized that I may not remember Him, but He will remember me."[2] The nun's transparent testimony is a good word for every trusting soul to keep in mind when headed to Mount Nebo.

Different people express their faith differently as they come to a promontory of Mount Nebo, a place in the soul's journey where the view of the Land of Promise is quite clear. If the Catholic Church asked me to nominate some Protestant for sainthood, I would lean strongly to William Wilberforce. British history remembers him as a member of Parliament who led the way through most of his rather long life to stop the slave trade and then to end slavery itself in Great Britain and the British colonies. But while this was his lifelong commitment, Wilberforce gave his time, his influence and his wealth to literally scores of other human needs—orphans of soldiers and sailors, a variety of ministries to the poor, educational projects for the disadvantaged, care for widows. Sir Reginald Coupland, the distinguished British historian, dared to say that "more than any man, [Wilberforce] had founded in the conscience of the British people a tradition of humanity and of responsibility towards the weak and backward."

Wilberforce dated his Christian life from the time of his conversion, as a young man, a conversion that touched every part of his life. Few persons have ever lived so consistent and devout a Christian life, much of it with people in positions of wealth and political influence who thought his fervor quite odd. In his hour of dying, in the midst of much physical suffering, he was reminded by his youngest son that his feet were "on the Rock." Wilberforce replied, "I do not venture to speak so positively, but I hope I have." It was the voice of humility. If one believes that salvation is the gift of grace, one will speak with faith but with careful recognition of the goodness that brings the other shore in view.

And what of heaven? The Scriptures speak of streets of gold and gates of pearl, a place where God "will wipe away every tear." "Death will be no more. There will be no mourning, crying, or pain anymore, for the former things have passed away" (Revelation 21:4). It is a place where God "is making all things news" (21:5).

Christians have used a variety of images and metaphors to describe heaven. It isn't surprising that a slave culture sang of a chariot that would "swing low" to carry them home, or of a place where they would "lay down my heaven load." Nor is it surprising that all of God's children got shoes, and all of God's children have a robe. A body of people whose wardrobe, if it may be called that, was of the barest essentials would see shoes and a robe as a more joyous symbol than streets of gold. I remember a sentimental song of my childhood, "When I Take My Vacation in Heaven." It spoke of a world where "so many" were taking vacations but where the song writer or the singer had no such privilege. No matter, a day was coming when there would be a vacation in heaven. Some will smile, of course, at such a naive picture of heaven. It seems more reflective than naive if one has lived with those who have never known even a week of paid vacation. The lyrics are not profound, but they come from the heart and they speak to the heart.

Most who talk about heaven, even if tentatively, think of it as a place of reunion. Some dare to ponder that perhaps they will have a chance to visit with some of the great souls of previous generations. Some even confess the questions they intend to present to Paul (let him now explain an obscure passage in an epistle) or to Mary Magdalene or King David. Such ruminations may lack gravity and may even seem rather presumptuous. Still, if three fishermen could sit in on a conversation between Jesus, Moses, and Elijah (Matthew 17:1-7), I don't want to pass judgment on conjectures that spring from deep human longing and simple trust.

Whatever our degree of presumed sophistication, our view of heaven—if we have one—tends to reflect our attitude toward this life. Several of the people I enjoy the most tell me that they think of heaven as a place of unending growth, a life where the human mind will come to its full, yet always expanding potential. It is said that on his death bed Leonardo da Vinci said, "It's too bad I am going to die. I'm just learning to paint." Some would say that heaven will give opportunity for the continued development of da Vinci and his painting, Bach and his music, Shakespeare and his writing. E. Stanley Jones, the iconic missionary, evangelist, and Christian statesman, said that when he got to heaven he would ask for twenty-four hours to rest, then twenty-four hours to visit with friends and renew old acquaintances. "Then I would like to go up to Jesus and say: 'This is wonderful, and I do not deserve to be here. But haven't you a world that is fallen, that needs an evangelist? Please send me.'"[3] For Dr. Jones, heaven is a chance to tell someone about Jesus Christ.

Several years ago when Kathleen Norris tried to define heaven she resorted to some grand sentences from Saint Augustine. I confirm her judgment.

> Let us sing alleluias here on earth, while we still live in anxiety, so that we may sing it one day in heaven in full security. . . . We shall have no enemies in heaven, we shall never lose a friend. God's praises are sung both here and there, but here they are sung in anxiety, there in security; here they are sung by those destined to die, there, by those destined to live forever; here they are sung in hope, there in hope's fulfillment; here they are sung by wayfarers, there, by those living in their own country. So then . . . let us sing now, not in order to enjoy a life of leisure, but in order to lighten our labors. You should sing as wayfarers do — sing, but continue your journey . . . Sing then, but keep going.[4]

The closing book of the New Testament, Revelation, tells us much about heaven, but above all this, that in heaven our occupation will be worship; that is, ultimate communion with God. Most of us ordinary mortals may wonder how we might manage in such a setting. Perhaps we have a hint in the Genesis story, in the paradise of Eden; we look now for a place of "day's cool evening breeze" (Genesis 3:8) where God walks among us. But in heaven, because we live in God's will and purpose, there will never have to fear of God's disapproval.

Even at its best our life on this earth is one where—as Robert Browning put it—our reach must exceed our grasp, "or what's a heaven for." We're almost certain to leave this life with some tasks unfinished, some dreams unfulfilled, some regrets still flying about the soul like a fly on a sweaty day. At times of such realization we should ask God's help to climb up Mount Nebo. Pausing there, look with grace and faith on the past, including days in the wilderness, then look off to God's heaven, and give thanks. Whatever this life has been, by God's grace and mercy, the best is yet to come.

NOTES

5. Grow Old Along with Me

1. *The Supplicating Voice: Spiritual Writings of Samuel Johnson* (New York: Vintage Books, 2005).

2. This John Donne thought originally appeared as Meditation 17 in 1624 in *Devotions Upon Emergent Occasions*.

3. Arthur John Gossip, *The Hero in Thy Soul* (New York: Kessinger, 2007), 227.

4. Ibid.

5. *Supplicating Voice*, 252.

6. Conrad Aiken, "Bread and Music."

8. Redeem the Time

1. Amy Bloom, "Getting Real," *AARP Magazine* (July-August 2008): 27.

2. Leon Danco, "Invest Time Wisely to Gain Big Dividends," *Crain's Small Business* (December 1994): S-5.

3. Joseph Epstein, *Narcissus Leaves the Pool* (Boston: Houghton Mifflin, 1999), 26.

4. Kilian McDonnell, *Swift, Lord, You are Not* (Collegeville, Minn.: St. John's University Press, 2003), 106.

9. I'm Not the Person I Used to Be

1. Barbara Mathias Riegel, "Why You Get the Joke," *AARP the Magazine*, (July-August 2004): 36. You can learn more about this concept in Barry Gordon and Lisa Berger, *Intelligent Memory* (New York: Viking Press, 2003).

2. Peter J. Gomes, *The Good Life* (New York: MarperOne, 2003), 148.

10. When the Shadows Are Dark and Deep

1. Joseph Sittler, *Gravity and Grace* (Minneapolis: Augsburg, 1986), 123.

2. R. R. Reno, "The Public Square," *First Things* (November 2011): 7.

3. John Tagliabue, "Walling Off Oscar Wilde's Tomb from Admirer's Kisses," *New York Times* (December 16, 2011): A6.

4. Clark Pinnock, e-mail message to Thomas Jay Oord, appears in entry "Pinnock, Alzheimer's, and Open Theology," *For the Love of Wisdom and the Wisdom of Love* Blog by Thomas Jay Oord, March 24, 2010, http://thomasjay oord.com/index.php/blog/archives/pinnock_alzheimers_and_open_theology/.

5. Peter Frick, ed., "I Believe," *Dietrich Bonhoeffer: Meditational Prayer* (Collegeville, Minn.: Order of Saint Benedict, 2010), 30.

11. There's More to Life Than Two Front Teeth

1. Marcus Tullius Cicero, *On the Good Life*, trans. Michael Grant (New York: Penguin Books, 1971).

2. Joseph Epstein, "Nobody Gets Out of Here Alive," *The Wall Street Journal* (January 29-30, 2011): C5.

3. Peter Gomes, *The Good Life* (New York: HarperOne, 2003), 137.

4. Kilian McDonnell, "Impatience at the Loom," *Swift, Lord, You are Not* (Collegeville, Minn.: Saint John's University Press, 2003), 23.

5. Dorothy Rowe, *Why We Lie: The Source of Our Disasters* (London: HarperCollins UK).

12. The Best Is Yet to Come

1. Helen Smith Shoemaker, *I Stand by the Door* (New York: Harper & Row, 1967), xi.

2. David Snowdon, *Aging with Grace* (New York: Bantam, 2001), 125.

3. E. Stanley Jones, *A Song of Ascents* (Nashville: Abingdon Press, 1968), 370.

4. Kathleen Norris, *Amazing Grace: A Vocabulary of Faith* (New York: Penguin, 1998), 368.

Discussion Guide for
I Love Growing Older, But I'll Never Grow Old
by J. Ellsworth Kalas

Chapter 1
I Love Growing Older, But . . .

Snapshot Summary

This chapter introduces us to this book about the joys and challenges to the process of growing older. It encourages us to fall in love with growing older and shows how it can become an exciting journey with God.

Reflection / Discussion Questions

1. Share your interest in this topic and what you hope to gain from reading this book and participating in this small group discussion.
2. When you were young, what thoughts did you have of older adults and growing older? What age did you consider as being "old" then and now?
3. Discuss the difference between growing older and growing old.
4. List some of the advantages of growing older.

5. Why should we think effectively and productively about growing older?

6. What does the author say about the audience for this book? Who should read it and why?

7. Why is it important to make peace with where you are right now? How can this help you enjoy growing older?

8. Discuss some of the financial and physical aspects of growing older.

9. Why should you fall in love with growing older?

Prayer
Dear God, thank you for each and every moment of this wonderful gift of life. Help us to look at growing older as an opportunity to grow closer to you, enjoy our time with others, and learn more about ourselves. Amen.

Chapter 2
There's Still Fruit in Old Age

Snapshot Summary
This chapter uses Psalm 92 as a reminder we can produce fruit at any age. It also looks at the lives of Caleb, Abraham and Moses in the Bible and shows how they flourished as they walked with God in their later years.

Reflection / Discussion Questions

1. Discuss the insights contained in Psalm 92:12-14.
2. Who do we become more introspective and retrospective? Is this good? How can it help us?
3. Why is it common to fear being a burden to others in older years?
4. "We need to invest in those virtues and qualities of person and character that make us nice to be around." List some of them.
5. Discuss what the Bible says of the later years of Abraham, Sarah and Moses.
6. What lessons can we learn from Caleb and his life?
7. Share your thoughts on what it means to believe in aging well.
8. Discuss the essence of right living.
9. List ways we can bear fruit as we grow older.

Prayer

Dear God, thank you for showing us we are always useful to you and others at any age. Help us to continue to bear fruit. Show us how to grow older without growing old. Amen.

Chapter 3
"There's No Fool Like an Old Fool"

Snapshot Summary

This chapter offers warnings and stories of how people can end up playing the fool as they grow older. It gives us examples from the Bible of aged foolishness. Topics include the dangers of harboring a grudge, the benefits of remembering our past, and how to protect ourselves from foolishness as we grow older.

Reflection / Discussion Questions

1. Share a time you felt like a young or old fool.
2. How can other people help us lose our judgment?
3. How was King Uzziah an example of aged foolishness?
4. What lessons and warnings are there in the life of King David?
5. Discuss the dangers of harboring a grudge.
6. How did Solomon play the fool? What can we learn from his life?
7. Discuss how we can protect ourselves from foolishness as we grow older.
8. List some of the benefits in remembering our past.
9. Why is growing older a lovely gift?

Prayer

Dear God, thank you for loving us even when we are foolish and make dumb mistakes. Protect us from foolishness as we grow older. Grant us wisdom to know right from wrong. Help us to trust and love you. Amen.

Chapter 4
By All Means, Go Home Again

Snapshot Summary

This chapter offers encouragement to re-visit your past, where you once lived, and the old familiar areas of your youth. It looks at sacred places, consorting with old ghosts, and shows how to be a beneficiary of your past.

Reflection / Discussion Questions

1. Discuss the meaning of the phrase, "You can't go home again."
2. Share your thoughts about your desire or lack of desire to go home again.
3. Name some places that are sacred to you.
4. Share a special memory about the neighborhood where you grew up as a child.
5. Discuss the connection between growing older and going home again.
6. What feelings come alive when you re-visit your past?
7. List the benefits of going home again.
8. Years later, how do you now view your old neighborhood and neighbors?

9. Name some images that come to mind as you remember your past and the homes you grew up in.

Prayer
Dear God, thank you for inviting us to go home again and to re-visit our past. Help us to learn from our past, to embrace it, and go forward creating new memories. Amen.

Chapter 5
Grow Old Along with Me

Snapshot Summary
This chapter uses the Robert Browning poem to begin a discussion of friendship and growing old with others. It shows how friends help improve your life and how to be a good friend to others.

Reflection / Discussion Questions
1. As you look back, share how friendships have enhanced your life.
2. Discuss the benefits of growing old with others.
3. List some of the gifts of getting older.
4. Discuss when we are most open to depth of friendship.
5. How are your best friends different from your other friends?

6. Discuss why people are more capable of true friendship in kindergarten and older years.
7. Why does the need for friendship increase with the passing of time?
8. List some qualities that make a good friend.
9. Explain how and why you need to be a friend to have a friend.

Prayer
Dear God, thank you for friends and the joys of friendship. Help us to be open to meeting new people, enjoying new experiences with them, and making new memories. Amen.

Chapter 6
If All Those Endearing Young Charms

Snapshot Summary
This chapter examines views on physical appearance as we grow older. It looks at why we don't want to look old, ways to remain young at heart, and how to age happily.

Reflection / Discussion Questions
1. Share your own thoughts on physical appearance.
2. Why is our devotion to "all those endearing young charms" greater than it has ever been?

3. Explain the statement: "We now live in the world of the forever young."
4. Why do you think the Bible says little about physical appearance and beauty?
5. Why don't we want to look old?
6. Explain what the author means by every face is a work in progress.
7. What can a face tell us about a person?
8. What did you learn about charm and its importance from this lesson?
9. How can we give God a chance to grow "endearing young charms" into enduring older charms?

Prayer

Dear God, thank you for reminding us about the realities of physical appearance. Help us to look our best, but be more concerned about how we feel inside than how we look outside. Show us how to value and strive for inner beauty. Amen.

Chapter 7
There Is Much Land Yet to Be Possessed

Snapshot Summary

This chapter uses Joshua 13:1 to show how productivity, learning and spiritual progress can continue as we grow older. It offers ideas of opportunities for later years and examines what the Apostle Paul said about goals and intentions.

Reflection / Discussion Questions

1. Share a special Bible verse and tell why it is a favorite.
2. What impresses you about how Joshua 13:1 touched the life of Dr. Kalas?
3. Why do many people become more spiritual as they grow older?
4. Discuss how growing older changes your priorities and values.
5. Why is it important to become intentional about your quest?
6. Discuss what Paul says about goals and intentions.
7. How can better time management help us make spiritual progress?
8. List ways to incorporate God's presence into other aspects of life.
9. Share your thoughts and ideas on the meaning of living a life that is full.

Prayer

Dear God, thank you for reminding us of new beginnings and opportunities that can be ours as we grow older. Help us to continue to make progress on our spiritual journey and to strive to live a life that is full and healthy. Amen.

Chapter 8
Redeem the Time

Snapshot Summary

This chapter helps us appreciate and make better use of time as God's priceless gift. It covers the importance of getting a sense of our mortality, and encourages investment in reading, relationships, travel and thinking.

Reflection / Discussion Questions

1. Discuss what it means to redeem your time.
2. Share an experience that helped you better appreciate the value of time.
3. Compare how young people and older people value time.
4. Discuss the value of getting a sense of our mortality.
5. How can we be more deliberate in choosing how our time is spent?
6. Discuss the value of investing time in relationships.
7. Why is it important to take time to read?
8. Discuss why travel is a good investment. List some benefits.
9. What are some of the benefits of investing more time in thinking?

Prayer

Dear God, thank you for the gift of time. Help us to use it wisely. Open our eyes to the many ways and opportunities to invest our minutes, hours, days and years. Amen.

Chapter 9
I'm Not the Person I Used to Be

Snapshot Summary

This chapter looks at how we change as we grow older. It encourages us to keep our potential alive, to build on the past one day at a time, and to reach toward the goal of growing up, not remaining young.

Reflection / Discussion Questions

1. Share a time you felt like you "were not the person you used to be."
2. Discuss why growing up isn't for wimps. Can you recall a specific time when your age provided a vantage point for you?
3. Did you ever have to abandon a dream? How did it feel?
4. Discuss why you should be glad you are not the person you used to be.
5. How do you take advantage of your memory?
6. Discuss the wisdom of building on your past, one day at a time.
7. Explain why the goal is to grow up, not to remain young.
8. Discuss how intelligent memory can improve with age.
9. How do we keep alive the joy of our human potential?

Prayer

Dear God, we thank you that we are not the person we used to be. Help us to continue to improve with age, build on our past, and grow in love toward you and others. Amen.

Chapter 10
When the Shadows Are Dark and Deep

Snapshot Summary

This chapter is about the troubles and problems that can come with growing older. It looks at financial and health challenges and shows how to cope with days of loss. We are reminded that faith in Christ is not only for days of sunshine, but also for stormy times.

Reflection / Discussion Questions

1. Name some of the dark and deep shadows that appear as you grow older.
2. Discuss what is meant by "the darkness of the valley depends partially on the vision of the traveler."
3. How do we learn from our fellow travelers about the dark shadows?
4. Share how it feels when all of life is a struggle.
5. Discuss the role "adjustments" play as you grow older.
6. Name some of the illnesses and diseases that can appear late in life and how people have coped with them.
7. How can God help you when the shadows are deep and dark?
8. Where do trust and faith come in as you grow older?
9. How can we prepare for the place of shadows?

Prayer

Dear God, thank you for being with us always, in the good and the not so good times of life. Help us face our struggles and challenges with dignity and the confidence that we are not in this alone. And may we also look for opportunities to help others in times of trial. Amen.

Chapter 11
There's More to Life Than Two Front Teeth

Snapshot Summary

This chapter reminds us that we have the capacity to enjoy life more as we grow older. We have a greater opportunity to do good. Our common sense increases as do many of our abilities. Even awareness of death can be a blessing as we age.

Reflection / Discussion Questions

1. Discuss why much of our best enjoyment of life is by way of comparison.
2. Why do we have a better capacity to enjoy life as we grow older?
3. Explain why what we lose as we grow older is often made up for by what we've gained.
4. Name some abilities that get better with age.

5. Discuss why those growing older have a greater capacity to do good.

6. How and why does common sense improve with age?

7. Why is it important to become a good listener?

8. How can prayer help you as you grow older?

9. Explain why awareness of death is a unique blessing.

Prayer

Dear God, thank you for our capacity to continue to enjoy life as we grow older. Help us to remember not what we have lost over the years, but what we have gained. And show us what you want us to accomplish today as we build on our past. Amen.

Chapter 12
The Best Is Yet to Come

Snapshot Summary

This final chapter provides lessons for us about life from the experiences of Moses and his Mount Nebo. It encourages us to believe in a bright future, to know God is with us, and that we can face any challenge.

Reflection / Discussion Questions

1. Share something about times in life when you wandered in the wilderness.

2. What can we learn from Moses about aging?
3. What should we do about choices and mistakes from our past that we can never mend?
4. Share your thoughts and beliefs about heaven.
5. Discuss why Samuel Johnson asked for innocence and usefulness.
6. What lessons can we learn from the life of William Wilberforce?
7. How can God help us climb our Mount Nebo?
8. Explain why the best is yet to come.
9. How have these lessons and discussions helped you?

Prayer

Dear God, thank you for reminding us that the best is yet to come. Help us to continue our journey with grace, faith and hope. Thank you for this group experience and all that was share. Be with us all, now and always. Amen.